WHEN PROTESTANTS ARGUE LIKE ATHEISTS

12 WEIRD WAYS THAT ANTI-CATHOLICS MIMIC SECULAR SKEPTICS

TRENT HORN

Published by Catholic Answers, Inc.
2020 Gillespie Way
El Cajon, California 92020
1-888-291-8000 orders
619-387-0042 fax
catholic.com

Printed in the United States of America

Cover design by ebooklaunch.com
Interior design by Russell Graphic Design

978-1-68357-313-5
978-1-68357-314-2 Kindle
978-1-68357-315-9 ePub

For John Paul

CONTENTS

INTRODUCTION

PURIFYING THE DISCUSSION

Where did I ever get the idea that Protestants argue like atheists? After all, I have much more in common with Protestants who affirm the existence of God and the divinity of Christ than I have with atheists who deny such truths. Strangely enough, it was a collaboration with a very like-minded Protestant that served as the inspiration for this book.

In August 2021, Cameron Bertuzzi, who was at that time a Protestant and host of the YouTube channel *Capturing Christianity*, asked me to debate an atheist at a conference he was hosting. Cameron's channel is dedicated to showing "the intellectual side" of Christianity and so I happily obliged. And before the conference started, I also agreed to sit down for an interview with Cameron about my Catholic faith.

As Cameron posed various challenges to Catholicism, I glanced over at Ben Watkins, the atheist I was going to be debating (who was waiting for Cameron to interview him as well). As I gave my answers, I noticed that Cameron's questions to me bore a striking resemblance to the questions I imagined Ben might ask Cameron about Christianity.

"If Protestantism is more modest [that is, simpler] in the claims that it makes," Cameron asked, "then isn't that one reason to prefer Protestantism over Catholicism?"

I replied, "I can see where you're coming from. Simpler explanations are often better than overly complex ones, but you don't want an explanation that is so simple that it creates more than problems than it solves."

I glanced over at Ben and then back at Cameron. "For example, one could argue that naturalism is simpler than theism—the claim God exists—because naturalism only proposes the natural world whereas theism says the natural *and* the supernatural exist. But even if naturalism were simpler, it leaves too many things unexplained to be the best framework for understanding reality. I think Protestantism suffers from a similar problem in explaining Christian revelation."

After that interview, I explored the question "Do Protestants argue like atheists?" in a few episodes of my podcast *The Counsel of Trent.* (Cameron also explored the arguments for Catholicism, and he entered the Church two years later.) I said on my podcast that when Protestants criticize Catholicism, their arguments parallel ones that atheists use when trying to refute Christianity. And it makes sense such a parallel exists, because both debates can be summarized in a similar way. Protestants and atheists basically tell Catholics and Christians:

- we both agree on the existence of something (Scripture/the natural world);
- you say a disputed thing (Catholic authority/the Christian God) must exist because only it can explain the thing we agree about;

- I disagree with that conclusion;
- there is not enough evidence to support the existence of the disputed thing (Catholic authority/the Christian God);
- there is even evidence that *contradicts* the existence of the disputed thing (biblical contradictions to Catholic teaching/the problem of evil and divine hiddenness).

As I continued to research these parallel arguments, I saw that my conclusions wouldn't just be an aid to Catholic apologetics. They would also help Protestants abandon arguments against Catholicism that could be used against Christianity if one merely swapped out a few of the argument's key terms (like *virgin Mary* for *risen Son*).

So that's what I'm trying to do in this book. But let me also make it clear what I am *not* trying to do. I am *not* saying:

- **Protestants are morally equivalent to atheists.** Just because two groups use similar arguments doesn't mean they have much, or anything, else in common. Protestants are fellow Christians, and the *Catechism of the Catholic Church* (CCC) says those "who believe in Christ and have been properly baptized are put in a certain, although imperfect, communion with the Catholic Church" (838). My sincere desire is for all Christians to be united in perfect communion with Christ's universal (i.e., Catholic) Church. Note also that when I use phrases like *Catholics and Christians* or *Catholicism and Christianity* I don't mean these are two separate religions. The religion of Christianity includes all people with valid baptisms.
- **Protestants are all the same.** The only doctrines all Protestants have in common (beyond "mere Christian"

beliefs like trinitarian theism) are their rejections of specifically Catholic doctrines, such as the papacy. So, when I speak about "Protestants" in this book, I understand that the term refers to a diverse movement whose own members do not agree on what counts as being "Protestant." That means that not every one of my criticisms will apply to every person who calls himself a Protestant, but many of them (or at least a variant of them) will, and so they're worth discussing.

- **Protestants are the only ones who argue like atheists.** I have tried throughout this book to engage in self-reflection and point out where Catholics, too, use these bad arguments and should stop doing it.

In that respect, I hope to *purify* the discussion between Catholics and Protestants, so that we can get to the root of the issues that divide us without getting stuck debating secondary issues using arguments we both would reject if an atheist were to present them to us. That's why I've enjoyed sharing these arguments with Protestant friends and dialoguing about them with Protestant guests on my podcast. It is my sincere goal that, even 500 years after the Reformation, this work can help Catholics and Protestants heed the word of the Lord found in the prophet Isaiah: "Come now, let us reason together" (Isa. 1:18).

1

THE BURDEN OF PROOF

"Why should I be Catholic?"

When Protestants ask this, a Catholic might be tempted to pull out a plethora of prooftexts to show how the Bible or the Church Fathers prove Catholicism is true. And although this can be helpful, sometimes I prefer a different approach. I might say,

"I'm happy to give you some reasons to be Catholic, but before I do that, I'm curious: Why are you Protestant?"

"Well, because I don't believe in the papacy and I don't believe Mary was without sin and . . ."

"Right, I understand why you aren't Catholic. But that doesn't answer my question. Why are you *Protestant*?"

But isn't a Protestant just a Christian who is not Catholic? (Or Eastern Orthodox, but for simplicity I will just say *Catholic*.) The problem with this definition is that Protestantism is more than just the absence of Catholicism. It makes specific claims about reality that carry their own burdens of proof. In other words, *disproving Catholicism doesn't prove Protestantism.*[1]

Arguing that Protestantism is merely a "lack of belief in Catholicism" parallels the popular atheist retort that atheism is merely a "lack of belief in theism." Protestants point out that atheism (and especially naturalism) makes positive claims about the world like "God does not exist" or "there is no reality beyond the natural world."

Just as Protestants rightfully insist that atheists have the burden of proving how a comprehensible universe exists apart from an infinite God who readily explains it, Protestants have the burden of proving how a comprehensible Christian revelation exists apart from an authoritative Church that readily explains it.

PROVING A "UNIVERSAL NEGATIVE"

Some atheists say that since we all agree the natural world exists, and theists claim that a disputed thing exists beyond the natural world (or God), then the burden is on the theist to prove the disputed thing exists. In a debate with Protestant philosopher William Lane Craig, the atheistic philosopher John Shook said, "An atheist is reasonable because no argument for supernaturalism is strong enough. The burden of proof about God is entirely on the theologian's shoulders."[2] But this is similar to Protestants who say that it is reasonable to believe Scripture is the only infallible rule of faith because no argument for another infallible rule of faith (like Sacred Tradition or the Church) is "strong enough." The burden of proof is entirely on the Catholic to prove his Church has divine authority alongside Scripture.

In addition, atheists claim that asking them to prove that God does *not* exist would force them to prove a "universal negative," which they say is impossible. Atheist Susan Jacoby says, "Of course an atheist can't prove there isn't a God, because you cannot prove a negative. The atheist basically says that, based on everything I see around me, I don't think so."[3]

You *can* prove a negative. You can prove, for instance, there isn't an elephant in your living room by just looking in it. Jacoby might mean that you can't prove certain kinds of *universal* negatives. For although one could prove through the definition of the words that there are no "square circles" or "married bachelors," it doesn't seem like you could just as easily prove that "there are no pink elephants." Even if you searched every place on earth and found no pink elephants, there could be some on a planet on the other side of the universe. In that case, all we can say about pink elephants is "based on everything I see around me, I don't think so."

This same complaint about disproving a "universal negative" can be seen in Protestant debates over *sola scriptura*. Consider what James White said in his 1996 debate with Catholic apologist Patrick Madrid:

> Now some opponents of *sola scriptura* have engaged in what can only be called cheap debating tricks in attempting to force the defender of scriptural sufficiency to prove a universal negative. That is, the less honest debater might attempt to force me to prove the non-existence of another rule of faith since I am saying that Scripture is unique in its function as the rule of faith of the Church. Some might challenge me to demonstrate that no other rule of faith could possibly exist. To illustrate this, I call your attention to my pen. Yes, to my pen. If our debate this evening was that I was going to stand here and say this is the only pen of its kind in all the universe, how would I go about proving it? Well, the only way I could prove

> the statement "there is no other pen like this in all the universe" is if I looked in all of your purses and all of your shirt pockets.[4]

White goes on to say that he would have to search the entire universe to prove that his pen is the only one of its kind. And since that's an absurd request, it follows that those who say other pens like his exist must prove that's true by producing such a pen. He has no burden of proving there are no other pens like his "one of a kind" pen. When applied to Scripture, the argument takes the following form:

- Scripture is the only infallible rule of faith.
- In order to prove there is no other infallible rule of faith (i.e., *sola scriptura*), one would have to search the entire universe for another infallible rule of faith.
- That's an absurd request.
- Therefore, the one who says Scripture is *not* the only infallible rule of faith (i.e. denies *sola scriptura*) must prove the existence of another infallible rule of faith.

But this sounds like a common argument that atheists make. You could put the argument this way:

- Natural things are the only kinds of things that exist.
- In order to prove there are no supernatural things, one would have to search the entire universe.
- That's an absurd request.

- Therefore, the one who says natural things are not the only kinds of things must prove the existence of a supernatural thing (i.e., God).

Each of these arguments begins with the assumption that a certain thing (a pen, Scripture, the natural world) is the only member of a certain kind (special pens, an infallible rule of faith, existing things). But these arguments are flawed because the assumption in their first premises is never *proved*.

Instead, the argument shifts the burden of proof by saying, "The only way to prove I'm wrong is to produce another special pen, another infallible rule of faith, or another thing that exists beyond the natural world." Greg Koukl does the same in this statement: "When I affirm *sola scriptura* . . . that claim itself is not meant to be an inerrant claim. [It] is meant to be a claim based on reflection on the nature of the Bible and other competing authorities."[5]

In other words, Koukl assumes that Scripture is an infallible authority and then concludes that Scripture is the *only* infallible authority because no other infallible authority has been proven to exist. But how is that different from a naturalist who says 1) the natural world exists; 2) no other, *super*natural thing has been proven to exist; 3) therefore *only* the natural world exists? In his book *Stealing from God: Why Atheists Need God to Make Their Case*, Frank Turek writes,

> Everyone has the burden of proof to support his or her position. Atheists must make a positive case that only material things exist. That's why instead of debating "does God exist?" I prefer to debate the question, "What better explains reality: atheism or theism?" Then it's obvious that both debaters have the burden of proof to support

their position. Atheists can't just identify what they think are deficiencies in theism.[6]

Catholics can borrow Turek's argument and apply his same reasoning to Protestantism:

> Everyone has the burden of proof to support his or her position. Protestants must make a positive case that Scripture is not just *an* infallible rule of faith, but that it is the *only* infallible rule of faith. That's why instead of debating "Is Catholicism true?" I prefer to debate the question "What better explains revelation: Protestantism or Catholicism?" Then it's obvious that both debaters have the burden of proof to support their position. Protestants can't just identify what they think are deficiencies in Catholicism.

Turek also says that atheists can only argue against God (for example, by saying that the God of the Bible is evil) by using parts of reality that only God explains. He writes, "These aspects of reality are so much [a] part of our common sense that many atheists seem to take them for granted. But they simply can't exist if atheism is true. Theism can explain them, but atheism cannot."[7] Similarly, Greg Koukl says, "Atheism is a physicalist system that does not have the resources to explain a universe thick with nonphysical things like moral obligations."[8]

By that same logic, we could say, "Protestantism is a system of written authority that does not have the resources to explain a revelation thick with non-written authorities like the canon of Scripture." And when Protestants use Scripture to say that Catholic doctrine is unbiblical, they resemble atheists who use objective morality to say that God is immoral. Protestants and atheists both appeal to parts of reality that they, as Turek says, take for granted as part of common sense. However, they don't realize that they are unable to explain why these parts of reality exist apart from the foundational reality (God/the Church) they are using those parts to argue against.

AGNOSTIC HAS JOINED THE CHAT

This brazen shifting of the burden of proof becomes obvious when we invite an *agnostic* into the discussion. As Protestant Paul Copan puts it, "In the absence of evidence for God's existence, agnosticism, not atheism, is the logical presumption. Even if arguments for God's existence do not persuade, atheism should not be presumed because atheism is not neutral; pure agnosticism is."[9]

The agnostic can say he doesn't know how many or *if any* special pens, infallible rules of faith, or purely natural things exist. If you want him to believe that the Bible is the only infallible rule of faith or that the natural world is all that exists, then you'll have to 1) prove the Bible is *an* infallible rule of faith/that the natural world exists and 2) prove the Bible is the *only* infallible rule of faith/*only* the natural world exists.

The idea of someone being agnostic about the existence of God makes sense, and you may even know a few people who identify as agnostics rather than atheists. But how could someone be "agnostic" about Catholicism and Protestantism? I admit there is only one person I've ever met who would count as such a person—myself, but it is enough to prove my point.

C.S. Lewis popularized the idea of a "mere Christian" as someone who is Christian but doesn't belong to any particular denomination. A mere Christian believes that which "has been common to nearly all Christians at all times" including that "there is one God and that Jesus Christ is his only Son."[10] William Lane Craig also defends "mere Christianity" and says that "belief in Christ's deity, atoning death, and resurrection would seem to be among the cardinal doctrines which any informed person must believe for salvation. Beyond these central truths, there just don't seem to be many other doctrines which are, so to speak, 'above the cutoff line.'"[11]

When I was in high school, William Lane Craig and C.S. Lewis's philosophical and historical arguments convinced me that God exists, that he became the man Jesus Christ, and that Christ rose from the dead. Upon believing these truths, I was "a Christian a who lacked a belief in Catholicism" but you would have been hard-pressed to call me a *Protestant*.

Up to this point, I assumed that the Bible was just a collection of human writings that communicated enough information to make it reasonable to believe Jesus was divine and rose from the dead. But when I recognized Jesus' divine identity, I didn't instantly shed my belief that the Bible was just a bunch of human writings. I still lacked a belief in a sixty-six-book Protestant canon of inspired, inerrant Scripture. I also lacked a belief in those scriptures being "the only infallible rule of faith" (the doctrine of *sola scriptura*).

If I had continued to treat the Bible as a helpful yet non-authoritative guide to Christianity, I doubt most Protestants would have counted me among their ilk. However, I quickly affirmed (or rather assumed) those "mere Protestant" beliefs about the Bible—but only because I was now a Christian. I did it simply because when I looked at other people who believed in Jesus, I saw they also had a typical belief about the Bible. But as my investigation continued, I realized that I was being inconsistent.

I followed many careful arguments before I felt confident enough to conclude that God existed or that Christ rose from the dead. But I didn't follow any similar chain of arguments before I concluded the Bible was a specific collection of inspired, inerrant books. I just noticed that every other Christian believed that; so why shouldn't I do the same? At that point in my conversion, Protestantism was my default position because I still wasn't convinced that Catholicism was true. But this view is only tenable if the Catholic/Protestant debate is framed in this way:

> Protestantism = I lack a belief in an infallible rule of faith beyond Scripture
>
> Catholicism = I believe there is an infallible rule of faith beyond Scripture

But this is as faulty as framing the debate on the existence of God in terms of people having or not having a "lack of belief in God":

> Atheism = I lack a belief in a supernatural reality beyond the natural world
>
> Theism = I believe there is a supernatural reality beyond the natural world

In either case, the debate should be over claims about the way reality *actually is* rather than how we feel about it. That means the debate over the existence of God should be framed this way:

> Atheism = There is no supernatural reality beyond the natural world
>
> Theism = There is a supernatural reality beyond the natural world

Agnosticism = I don't know if there is a supernatural reality beyond the natural world

And the debate over the nature of Christian revelation should be framed in this way:

Protestantism = There is no infallible rule of faith beyond Scripture

Catholicism = There is an infallible rule of faith beyond Scripture

Mere Christianity = I don't know if there is an infallible rule of faith

STEALING FROM GOD—AND TRADITION?

You may have noticed in my comparison that the analogy has slightly broken down, but not in a way that helps Protestantism become more tenable.

The atheist, agnostic, and theist all agree the natural world exists and trust their sense perception to justify that claim. They can easily cross the gap that exists between the self-evident claim "I exist" and the fairly obvious claim "the universe exists." But while Catholics and Protestants agree "Scripture exists," the mere Christian who is agnostic about their authority claims doesn't even know if there is such a thing as inspired Scripture.

All three groups believe God exists and that he revealed himself through the miracles of Jesus Christ. Protestants go further and say there is one infallible authority in the form of Scripture and Catholics go even further in proposing infallible authority in Scripture, Tradition, and specific teachings of the Magisterium. While atheists and theists didn't have to prove the natural world exists to the agnostic, *both* Catholics and Protestants must show the mere Christian that their infallible authority exists.

If Protestants say the Bible is an infallible authority because it just *is* the word of God, then they're arguing in a circle. The same reasoning, after all, could justify claims of inspiration made about the Quran or the Book of Mormon. But if they appeal to a widespread acceptance of these books as inspired, inerrant Scripture, then they are "stealing from Tradition" to make arguments for Protestantism in the same way atheists "steal from God" in order to make arguments for atheism like the problem of evil. In other words, just as atheists who say evil proves God does not exist need God to explain how something can be "evil," Protestants who say the Bible disproves Sacred Tradition need Sacred Tradition to explain what writings constitute the Bible.

Moreover, Protestants often say it is inconsistent for atheists to say we can trust our intuitions about immaterial moral truths or immaterial minds existing but not our intuitions about God's existence. But by that same reasoning, it is inconsistent for Protestants to say we can trust traditions witnessed in the Church Fathers regarding the canon of Scripture but not similar, or even better attested traditions in those same writings about things like baptismal regeneration, bishops with apostolic succession, and the like.

So to summarize, just as atheists and theists both have to prove their claim that reality exists in a certain way, Catholics and Protestants both have to prove their claim that divine revelation exists in a certain way. But while atheists and theists can easily "cross the gap" from their existence to the existence of a universe that needs an explanation, Catholics and Protestants can't easily cross a similar gap from the existence of God to the fact of God revealing himself through specific writings.

Although, some Protestants *have* bravely attempted to cross the gap between mere Christianity and mere Protestantism, but the path they propose resembles a rickety suspension bridge you'd rather bypass if possible.

CAN PROTESTANTS CROSS THE GAP?

In *I Don't Have Enough Faith to Be an Atheist*, Protestant authors Norm Geisler and Frank Turek spend more than 300 pages defending the existence of God and the divinity of Christ, and about ten pages defending the authority of the New Testament. The first argument they give for the New Testament's authority is the claim that "[Jesus] said the New Testament would come through his apostles because the Holy Spirit would remind them what Jesus had said and would lead them into 'all truth.' This is recorded in two passages of John's Gospel." They then cite John 14:25–26, where Jesus promises to send the Holy Spirit who "will teach you all things," and John 16:12–13, where Jesus says the Spirit of Truth will "guide you into all truth."

What do these verses mean?

They claim: "Jesus is promising his apostles that the Holy Spirit would lead them to author what we now know as the New Testament. St. Paul would later echo this teaching of Jesus by asserting that the Church is 'built on the foundation of the apostles and prophets, with Christ Jesus himself as the chief cornerstone' [Eph. 2:20]."[12]

Conspicuously absent from these or *any* Scripture verses are references to Jesus or the apostles promising there would be a written collection of books that would be the Church's sole, infallible rule of faith (or even *a* rule of faith). Geisler and Turek simply assume that phrases like "all truth" or "founded on the apostles" mean a collection of writings from the apostolic age. They cite a few places in the New Testament that describe other writings as "Scripture," but none of those passages speaks about the Church having an authoritative list of books that will be a believer's "sole, infallible rule of faith."

When Geisler and Turek discuss how we know what writings constitute "Scripture," they say, "The only books that should be part of the New Testament are those that God has inspired. Since Jesus said that his apostles would produce those books, our only questions are historical: 1) Who were the apostles? and 2) What did they write?" They also add the criteria that the authors of an inspired work must have performed a miracle in order to authenticate their message. Or as they put it, "Those apostles had been confirmed by miracles," and "The miracle confirms the message. The sign confirms the sermon."[13]

There is no historical basis, however, for this criterion of the New Testament canon.

Jesus never spoke of his disciples "producing books." Prior to his ascension into heaven, Jesus never told *anyone* to write *anything* down. More distressing than the absence of evidence for this criterion is the evidence against it. Specifically, it can't be used as an objective standard to reconstruct the New Testament canon.

For example, if the author of an inspired text must be a miracle-worker, then only the works of Peter and Paul would be inspired, since the New Testament doesn't say that other apostolic authors, like Matthew, James, Jude, and John, performed miracles. And if the author must be an apostle, then this would disqualify Mark, Luke, and the anonymous author of Hebrews.

Perhaps this is why Geisler and Turek qualify their meaning of "apostolic authorship" and include the ambiguous descriptor "those confirmed by the apostles." And how do we know who these people were? Geisler and Turek tell us that "there is an unbroken chain of testimony from the apostles to the early Church fathers regarding the authorship and authenticity of the New Testament books."[14] They then note that twenty-six of the twenty-seven books of the New Testament are cited across Apostolic Fathers like Sts. Polycarp, Ignatius, Clement, and Irenaeus.

However, no single Father cites all of these books, and the majority of these citations are just that—citations. The Fathers also cite non-canonical first-century works like the Shepherd of Hermas, the book of Enoch (including it as Scripture) and First Clement. A citation, in itself, does not prove that the source was viewed as authoritative (indeed, even the Bible cites Enoch: in Jude 14–15). It can be viewed this way if the citation describes the work as "Scripture" or uses it to prove doctrine. But this further muddles Geisler and Turek's argument, because the Apostolic Fathers cite the deuterocanonical books of the Old Testament in this way but Geisler, Turek, and other Protestants reject those books!

The holes in Geisler and Turek's approach shows that their defense of the New Testament canon commits the *Texas sharpshooter fallacy.*

That name comes from a joke about the greatest gunslinger in Texas, who randomly fires rounds into the side of a barn and then paints targets around the tightest concentrations of hits while ignoring the other widely scattered bullet holes. The fallacy occurs when a person imposes a narrow pattern over a wide range of data in order to support a particular conclusion.

In Geisler and Turek's case, the fallacy occurs because they already believe in their authority for "mere Protestantism"—a collection of twenty-seven inspired, inerrant books composed (or confirmed) by miracle-working apostles. They begin with that pattern in mind and then they scour the writings of the first Christians in order to find places where the pattern is confirmed. But instead of painting targets, they reference where the Church Fathers cite the New Testament writings. And instead of ignoring scattered bullet holes, they downplay Fathers who did not cite certain New Testament books and ignore Fathers who cited non-biblical works as Scripture.

If you looked at the earliest, non-biblical Christian writings and had no previous knowledge of the biblical canon, you'd have no idea these authors believed in the canon Turek and Geisler defend. They used the word *inspired* (*theopneustos*) to describe biblical and non-biblical texts, and according to Baptist scholar Lee Martin McDonald, "The notion of a closed New Testament canon was not a second-century development in the early church, and there were still considerable differences of opinion about what should comprise that canon even in the fourth and fifth centuries."[15]

WHEN CATHOLICS ARGUE LIKE ATHEISTS

Even if Protestants can't successfully cross the "gap" between mere Christianity and minimal Protestantism (a sixty-six-book canon governed by *sola scriptura*), that doesn't mean Catholics have proven their case by default. Each side has to carry the burden of proof; when Catholics refuse to do this, they argue like atheists, too. This isn't always intentional, but it can happen when Catholics use simplistic means to cross the gap between mere Christianity and Catholicism.

For example, I've seen tee-shirts, posters, and internet memes compare the founders of various Protestant denominations going all the way back to Martin Luther in 1517. They then jump down to A.D. 33 and state that "Jesus

Christ founded the Catholic Church." I admit it is amusing to type into a search engine, "Who founded the Catholic Church?" or to ask an AI assistant the same question, and get an answer like "Jesus Christ" or "St. Peter," but this isn't going to impress a serious Protestant. Catholics must also cross the gap between mere Christianity and Catholicism—they can't merely *assume* that their Church has a historical continuity going back to the apostles and that it simply "gave us the Bible."

Consider this challenge from Protestant scholar Michael Kruger: "How does the Roman Catholic Church establish its *own* infallible authority? If the Roman Catholic Church believes that infallible authorities (like the scriptures) require external authentication, then to what authority does the church turn to establish the grounds for its own infallible authority?"[16]

Kruger is correct that every authority claim does not need to be established by another authority claim—this would create an infinite regress. And neither Catholics nor Protestants are justified in stopping the regress by simply assuming that their structure of authority is self-evident. But since Catholicism is not constrained by a doctrine like *sola scriptura*, it has more resources to determine what is the canon of Scripture: such as the teaching office of the Church, manifested in different ways through the regional and ecumenical councils that confirmed that these books were inspired.

Catholics can also appeal to early Christian writings, both biblical and non-biblical, as historical witnesses to Jesus and the apostles establishing an authoritative, hierarchical, and enduring Church. For example, Ignatius of Antioch (writing c. A.D. 110) tells Christians to "do nothing apart from the bishop"[17]; Clement of Rome (A.D. 60–96) describes the apostles choosing successors[18]; and Irenaeus (A.D. 180) says of the church at Rome that "it is a matter of necessity that every church should agree with this church, on account of its preeminent authority" and gives a list of the successors of the bishop of Rome.[19]

It is beyond the scope of this book to comprehensively describe all of the evidence for the Church's authority in the earliest Christian writings (though I have addressed that evidence in other works). Instead, my point is simply that we should compare the earliest Christian witnesses, biblical and non-biblical, and honestly ask what authority structure they envision. Is it a specific set of writings that explicitly rules out other infallible authorities (*sola scriptura*), or is it sacred writings, sacred oral tradition, and the teaching authority of the successors of the apostles? Once again, McDonald admits that, when it comes to early Fathers like Irenaeus,

> The establishing of a closed canon of inspired scriptures, however, was not Irenaeus's primary concern, but rather to defend the Christian message with all the tools at his disposal. He sought to root his teaching in the apostolic teaching and tradition that, he argued, was passed on in the church through the succession of bishops as well as by the authority of both the Old Testament and New Testament.[20]

2

SOLA SCRIPTURA AND "SOLA SCIENCIA"

"Where is that in the Bible?"

This is the most common question I receive when I discuss the Catholic faith with Protestants. They ask me questions like: "Where is purgatory in the Bible? Or the Mass? Or the pope? Or the rosary?"

These questions assume that Christians should only believe a doctrine if it is explicitly taught in Scripture—what is called *sola scriptura* ("by Scripture alone"). The 1647 Protestant Westminster Confession of Faith expressed a key aspect of *sola scriptura* this way: "The whole counsel of God, concerning all things necessary for his own glory, man's salvation, faith, and life, is either expressly set down in Scripture, or by good and necessary consequence may be deduced from Scripture."[21]

Now, for many questions I actually can point to explicit biblical evidence for Catholic beliefs and practices. But I consider it more fruitful to challenge the assumption behind the attitude, "I won't believe it unless you can prove it from Scripture alone." From my perspective, it sounds a lot like when atheists tell me, "I won't believe it unless you can prove it from *science* alone."

In both cases, the person I'm engaging has adopted a standard for determining what is true that not only fails to account for some of our most basic beliefs—it ends up refuting itself. In fact, some of the best arguments against *sola scriptura* can be adapted from Protestant criticisms of *scientism*, or the belief that we should only believe what can be known from "science alone."

SOLA SCRIPTURA IN THE "TRUTH BOX"

The Protestant author Greg Koukl says the claim that "science is the only reliable method of knowing truth about the world" defeats itself or that it "self-destructs." He writes:

> Imagine you wanted to collect all knowledge in a box. Let's call it the "Truth Box." Before any alleged truth could go into the box it must first pass the scientific truth test (the claim of scientism). The problem is that your knowledge project could never get started because some truths need to be in the Truth Box first before science itself could begin its analysis.[22]

Koukl says these include foundational truths about math, logic, and the reliability of our senses. It even includes moral principles like "report all data honestly." Most importantly, he says, "the entire scientific method must be in the box before the method itself can be used to test the truthfulness of anything else."

But if Protestants say nothing can enter the "Christian Truth Box" unless it passes the "scriptural truth test," they will have the same problem: the claim that "all doctrine must be found in Scripture," not to mention the definition of *Scripture* itself, would already need to be in the box. Since this is self-defeating, our knowledge of Christian doctrine cannot come from Scripture alone.

Interestingly, in an online video Koukl takes up the challenge that *sola scriptura* is self-refuting. He says this would be the case if you defined *sola scriptura* as the claim that "only the Bible has truth." Koukl says the Bible would have to "fulfill its own requirements" and contain this specific statement. However, Koukl maintains that *sola scriptura* makes the more modest claim that Scripture is "the only source of inerrant authority" and so this isn't self-refuting.[23]

But remember that Koukl's definition of a self-refuting scientism was *not* "Only science has truth." It was "Science is the only *reliable* method of knowing truth about the world." People who defend "scientism" might admit there are truths we can know that are not scientific in nature (such as testimonial truths about history). But if there's any dispute among those other ways of knowing, science must settle it—because science is the only reliable way of discovering truth about the world.

Defenders of *sola scriptura* have adopted a similar framework by arguing that *sola scriptura* does not mean that "all doctrine comes from Scripture." Instead, it means that "the Bible is the only infallible rule of faith" or, as Koukl says, "the only source of inerrant authority." They say that Sacred Tradition or Church councils are indeed authorities and rules of faith, but if there's any dispute between them, Scripture must settle it—because Scripture is the most reliable means of establishing Christian doctrine. The nineteenth-century Reformed theologian Charles Hodge said, "All Protestants agree in teaching that 'the word of God, as contained in the Scriptures of the Old and New Testaments, is the only infallible rule of faith and practice.'"[24]

The problem with these "moderate" formulations of *sola scriptura* and "*sola sciencia*" is that there isn't a meaningful difference between something being the "only infallible" or "only reliable" rule and something being the "only" rule (or only sole source) of knowledge.

Koukl's critical characterization of scientism was that anything that goes into our "truth box" (our collection of beliefs) must first pass through the filter of science or receive scientific confirmation. Even if less reliable forms of knowledge are used to acquire truths, they must still be approved by "the only reliable rule of knowledge": science. But this is just a roundabout way of saying that *the only things we can know are what science tells us.* And this requirement of using a "scientific filter," as well as our knowledge of how such a filter would even work, can't be confirmed in this way, so it's self-refuting.

The same thing happens to Koukl's modified definition of *sola scriptura.* If all Christian doctrine must pass through the filter of "Scripture alone," even if it is acquired through other means (like the decrees of ecumenical councils), then this is just a roundabout way of saying that *the only doctrines we can know are those contained in Scripture.* And by that reasoning, we would have to put the concept of "Scripture" and the method of "Scripture alone" through the same filter—but we can't, so it fails just as scientism's "truth box" fails.

WHAT SCIENCE AND SCRIPTURE CAN'T TELL US

In their book *I Don't Have Enough Faith to Be an Atheist,*

Protestant authors Frank Turek and Norm Geisler show that scientism is false not only because it is self-refuting, but because it can't justify our knowledge of many things we know to be true.

The duo recount attending a debate between William Lane Craig and Peter Atkins on the existence of God, at which Atkins asked Craig, "Do you deny that science can account for everything?" Craig confidently answered that he did deny it, because science can't account for statements about math, logic, ethics, aesthetics, and even science itself. Turek and Geisler agree with him, adding, "The scientific method of searching for causes by observation and repetition is but *one* means of finding truth. It is not the *only* means of finding truth."[25]

But if scientism can be refuted with knowledge of reality acquired apart from science, then *sola scriptura* can be refuted with knowledge of Christian doctrine acquired apart from Scripture—including knowledge of what constitutes "Scripture."

Geisler also co-authored a critique of Catholicism called *Roman Catholics and Evangelicals: Agreements and Differences*. In it, he doesn't say that Scripture is but *one* means of finding truth about God's revelation. Instead, he says, "Scripture is the sufficient and final written authority of God. As to sufficiency, the Bible—nothing more, nothing less, and nothing else—is all that is necessary for faith and practice."[26] The Reformed theologian Matthew Barrett says something similar in his 2016 book *God's Word Alone*: "*Sola scriptura* means that only Scripture, because it is God's inspired Word, is our inerrant, sufficient, and final authority for the church. . . . All things necessary for salvation and for living the Christian life in obedience to God and for his glory are given to us in the scriptures."[27]

If Scripture is so utterly sufficient, can Geisler use it to answer the question "What human writings are Scripture?"

The answer seems to be no, because, instead of citing Scripture to answer that question, Geisler says that "the church is only a witness, not a judge of the canon, that is all books which the apostles and prophets wrote."[28] But the Bible never defines *Scripture* as "all books which the apostles and prophets wrote." The Old Testament contains books that were not written by prophets (e.g., Nehemiah), and the New Testament contains books not written by apostles (e.g., the Gospels of Mark and Luke).

Geisler also confidently says that "canonical revelation ceased at the end of first century," but he doesn't cite any Scripture to prove this point.[29] He merely says that this is something on which Catholics and Protestants agree. But this is like an atheist saying, "Rape is always wrong" and instead of showing why this is true, he just notes that the wrongness of rape is something on which atheists and Christians agree.

Christians will sometimes argue that atheists have no objective justification for their *feeling* that rape is always wrong. The fact that there is a common recognition that rape is wrong doesn't turn that recognition into an authority that *makes* rape wrong; therefore, some other authority is needed.

Likewise, Catholics will point out to Protestants that there is no objective justification for their feeling that public revelation ended in the first century. The fact that there is a common recognition that revelation has ceased doesn't turn that recognition into an authoritative teaching that binds Christians.

In both these cases, we must go deeper and seek the existence of something that grounds these commonly held beliefs and either makes them true (as in the case of the relationship between God and objective morality) or gives us certain knowledge they are true (as in the case of the relationship between Christ's Church and the limits of divine revelation).

But does elevating the authority of the Church diminish the authority of Scripture? After all, just as an atheist might say that once we abandon scientism we open ourselves up to all kinds of errors, a Protestant might say that once we abandon *sola scriptura* we open the door to all kinds of heresies.

However, rejecting scientism doesn't mean that science ceases to be an important standard. Thomas Aquinas said that if a physical theory about the world that comes from an interpretation of Scripture "can be shown to be false by solid reasons, [then] it cannot be held to be the sense of holy Scripture."[30] The *Catechism*, quoting the First Vatican Council, declares, "Though faith is above reason, there can never be any real discrepancy between faith and reason. Since the same God who reveals mysteries and infuses faith has bestowed the light of reason on the human mind, God cannot deny himself, nor can truth ever contradict truth" (159).

In other words, in order to understand reality we need non-scientific tools like philosophy and religious experience; and, when they are used properly, these tools do not contradict one another. Even if science isn't treated like the most or only reliable way of acquiring knowledge, it is still useful to keep us from adopting false, unscientific beliefs even if it can't prove all true beliefs.

In the same way, Catholics can assure Protestants that even though it is self-refuting to make Scripture "the only infallible rule of faith," that doesn't mean Scripture loses its authority. Catholics vigorously agree with Protestants that no doctrine can ever *contradict* Scripture even if it is not explicitly described in Scripture (e.g., infant baptism). Since not all doctrines are explicitly found in Scripture, we need non-scriptural "tools" like Sacred Tradition and the teaching office of the Church to understand them. When they are used properly, these tools do not contradict one another, or as the Second Vatican Council put it:

> The task of authentically interpreting the word of God, whether written or handed on, has been entrusted exclusively to the living teaching office of the Church, whose authority is exercised in the name of Jesus Christ. This teaching office is not above the word of God, but serves it, teaching only what has been handed on, listening to it devoutly, guarding it scrupulously and explaining it faithfully in accord with a divine commission and with the help of the Holy Spirit, it draws from this one deposit of faith everything which it presents for belief as divinely revealed (*Dei Verbum* 10).

AN OFFENSIVE AGAINST TRADITION

Atheists usually abandon scientism when they've been logically backed into a corner, but sometimes they still try to score rhetorical points by noting what science has gotten right and religion has gotten wrong. And when faced with the charge that *sola scriptura* is self-refuting, some Protestant apologists do something similar and attack the concept of Sacred Tradition.

They say that unwritten forms of revelation are less reliable than Scripture and so we can't have confidence in their conclusions. For example, in response to the claim that sacred apostolic traditions guided the early Church, Geisler says that "oral traditions are notoriously unreliable. They are the stuff of which legends and myths are made."[31]

Geisler sounds a lot different however, when he's defending the oral traditions that first constituted the writings of the New Testament. Non-religious critics like Bart Ehrman say the New Testament is unreliable because the transmission of oral traditions about Jesus were like the childhood game of telephone.[32] In response to this assertion, Geisler argues that

> since the New Testament writers were living in a culture where the vast majority of people were illiterate, there was no initial need for utility in writing [their testimonies] down. First-century people in Palestine, by necessity, developed strong memories in order to remember and pass on information. . . . In such an oral culture, facts about Jesus may have been put into a memorable form.[33]

And rather than portraying Scripture as God's singular plan of revelation for the Church (as Protestants do with Catholics), Geisler seems to downplay the need to write Scripture, choosing instead to defend the use of oral traditions about Jesus. For example, Geisler says the disciples may have expected Jesus to return soon and that "as they aged, perhaps they thought it wise to put their observations down on papyrus." He also says that once Christianity expanded throughout the Roman Empire, "time and distance forced the New Testament writers to write it down."[34]

Now, one might object that oral traditions about Jesus only had to survive for a few decades before they were recorded in Sacred Scripture but the same is not true for the apostolic traditions that guided the early Church. For example, the first written testimony by an early Christian writer attesting to the apostolic origin of infant baptism comes from the third-century writer Origen.[35] But there are earlier written accounts that attest to other apostolic traditions. For example, the first-century Letter of Clement describes how the apostles knew they would be persecuted so they chose successors for their ministry.[36]

Even if we granted this objection, it only saves New Testament traditions at the expense of traditions from the Old Testament. After all, the stories involving the Patriarchs (not to mention the primeval history in Genesis 1–11) existed for centuries as oral traditions before they were committed to writing. That's why Geisler defends the historical reliability of Old Testament accounts by saying, "Oral tradition was very important in the Jewish culture and served as one of the main ways to transfer information, among many other things."[37]

Geisler's standard for oral tradition, then, basically boils down to: *Jewish and Christian traditions good, Catholic traditions bad.*

ARGUMENTS FROM SILENCE AND COUNTERFEITS

Other Protestants ask a question that is supposed to stop Catholics in their tracks: "Is there any specific saying of Jesus or the apostles that has been infallibly preserved outside of Scripture?"

Most Catholics would say "no," but just because apostolic *words* have been recorded only in Scripture it doesn't follow that apostolic *truths* have been recorded only in Scripture. This question smuggles in the assumption that the only place to find apostolic truths is in the verbatim words of Jesus or the apostles.

Likewise, when atheists ask Christians, "In the history of science, has a supernatural explanation ever replaced a natural explanation?" it smuggles in the assumption that the only place to find truths about reality is through the scientific method.

Many non-Christians also claim that "Jesus never said anything about homosexuality" in order to cast doubt on the idea of this behavior being sinful. But Protestants don't take this to mean that Jesus never gave the apostles any *teachings* on the matter, even if the Bible doesn't record him discussing the subject. Alan Shlemon, a Protestant who works with Greg Koukl, says,

> It's not certain that Jesus never said anything about homosexuality. It's possible he did address it but his statement wasn't recorded. The Gospel writers didn't document everything Jesus said and did—only what they thought was important to their audience. Indeed, most of what Jesus said (and did) was never written down. John 21:25 says, "And there are also many other things which Jesus did, which if they were written in detail, I suppose that even the world itself would not contain the books that would be written." It's possible Jesus did talk about homosexuality but the Gospel writers didn't feel it was necessary to include it in their accounts.[38]

St. Paul also confirms that apostolic truths were passed on in a variety of forms when he exhorts the Thessalonians to "stand firm and hold to the traditions which you were taught by us, either by word of mouth or by letter" (2 Thess. 2:15).[39]

Another claim is that we have no idea what counts as Sacred Tradition and what doesn't. In his book *The Roman Catholic Controversy*, James White has a chapter entitled "The Thousand Traditions" and in his work *Scripture Alone* he rejects the reliability of apostolic Tradition because of the existence of false apostolic traditions. He cites the example of St. Irenaeus believing that Jesus was crucified at the age of fifty, which contradicts Scripture and is also not endorsed by any other Church Father. White continues, "It seems impossible to avoid concluding that if an allegedly apostolic Tradition can be corrupted in less than a century, how can we take seriously the claim of Rome that her Marian dogmas . . . are truly apostolic in origin and form?"[40]

But if counterfeit apostolic traditions disprove genuine apostolic traditions, then counterfeit apostolic writings would disprove genuine apostolic writings.

Skeptical scholars like Bart Ehrman note that in the early Church there were dozens of apocryphal gospels attributed to people like Peter, Phillip, Mary Magdalene, and Thomas (which Origen cites). The Gospel of Peter has been dated to the year 125, and so we see, to borrow White's language, that an "allegedly apostolic *writing* can be corrupted in less than a century." And this problem wasn't restricted to decades or centuries after the time of the apostles. Paul thought it necessary to warn his audience "not to be quickly shaken in mind or excited, either by spirit or by word, or by letter purporting to be from us" (2 Thess. 2:2).

The English word *tradition* comes from the Latin word *tradere*, which means "what is handed on." So, in one sense, Scripture is Tradition because it has been "handed on" to future generations. This is why Protestant attacks on Sacred Tradition are so dangerous: they risk eating away at the trustworthiness of *anything* the apostles handed on to the Church in the first century, including Scripture itself.

WHEN CATHOLICS ARGUE LIKE ATHEISTS

Studying science is a great way to understand the natural world and studying Scripture is a great way to understand God's revelation. When Protestants require scriptural proof before believing that something is divinely revealed, they act like atheists who require scientific proof before believing that something is an objective part of reality. But Catholics can also act like atheists when it comes to knowledge about the world—when they embrace a kind of self-defeating skepticism.

For example, some Catholics say that Protestantism is fatally flawed because there is no way an infallible Scripture can be everyone's ultimate authority. Instead, one's *fallible interpretation* of that Scripture will inevitably be the final authority. But given the conflicting opinions that Protestants have about the meaning of Scripture, a Protestant can never be certain he has the correct interpretation of it. Since an authority structure can't be built upon a fallible interpretation of God's word, they say, it must instead be built upon an infallible interpretation of it. And this is only found in the teaching office of the Catholic Church.

You could summarize the argument this way: an infallible text requires an infallible interpreter.

But just as it is self-defeating to require scientific proof for all truths, or biblical proof for all doctrines, it is self-defeating to require infallible certainty for all interpretative judgments. After all, a Protestant can rightly ask a Catholic who makes this argument, "If I can't trust my fallible judgment about what the Bible means, then how can you trust your fallible judgment about what various Church documents mean? Do you need an infallible interpreter in order to understand what the infallible interpreter said? Or, if you can fallibly recognize the Catholic Church's authority then why can't I fallibly arrive at the unique and sufficient authority of Scripture?"

No one can escape the need to make fallible judgments about what is true based on the nature of evidence. Protestants look at the evidence and make a decision to trust a model rooted in *sola scriptura*, and Catholics look at the same evidence and make a decision to trust a model rooted in Sacred Scripture, Sacred Tradition, and the Magisterium.

This is why I prefer the more modest argument I mentioned in the previous chapter, which avoids claims about "fallible judgments." Instead, it asks which of these judgments has the best chance of crossing the "gap" between the giving of divine revelation in the first century and the framework of Scripture and apostolic traditions that Christians use to understand that revelation. Catholicism is simply in a much better position to cross that gap because it allows for God to transmit his revelation through Sacred Tradition and the teachings of the Magisterium instead of relying on Scripture alone to determine its scope.

3

IRRESOLVABLE CONTRADICTIONS?

In the previous chapters, we saw that Catholicism's claim of having a historically continuous teaching authority going back to the apostles is an asset when it comes to explaining things like our knowledge of the canon of Scripture. It avoids the self-refuting nature of *sola scriptura* and awkward Protestant attempts to make early traditions on the canon normative while ignoring or rejecting other norms from the early Church (e.g., Catholic sacraments, apostolic succession vested in bishops, papal supremacy).

But some Protestants say this teaching authority is actually a liability for Catholics, because it provides numerous opportunities to falsify Catholicism. Jerry Walls, for example, says Catholic belief about the papacy having an apostolic origin grievously contradicts the historical record. He writes:

> Roman apologists are reminiscent of young-earth creationists who continue to assert that the earth is only 10,000

> years old in the face of the massive scientific evidence that it is much older, evidence which is acknowledged by leading Christian physicists and cosmologists, as well as other scientists. Popular apologists who continue to assert traditional papal history in the face of the best scholarship of their own church are doing the same sort of thing.[41]

Catholicism may *seem* to have excellent explanatory power, say these Protestants, but scholarship shows that Catholic teaching over the past 2,000 years contradicts itself or the historical record. And since the Church claims to have infallible teaching authority, it follows that Catholicism is false because infallible authorities can't be in error or contradict themselves.

Fortunately, Catholics have ample resources when it comes to answering this kind of argument—because atheists have been lobbing similar objections at Christianity for centuries.

UNDERSTANDING INERRANCY AND INFALLIBILITY

One common tactic among atheists is to say that the Bible can't be an infallible source of revelation because it is riddled with contradictions, and so Christianity is false. One nineteenth-century skeptic bombastically declared,

> The Bible contains errors of almost every description; historical errors, geographical errors, chronological errors, philosophical errors, grammatical errors, rhetorical errors, logical errors, theological errors, moral errors, prophetical errors, poetical errors, zoological errors, astronomical errors, and geological errors: errors, in short, of every description.[42]

The Church teaches that, when it comes to Sacred Scripture, "everything asserted by the inspired authors or sacred writers must be held to be asserted by the Holy Spirit" (*Dei Verbum* 11). Notice that the word *asserted* is used instead of *written*. Just because something is written in Scripture it doesn't mean the Holy Spirit is asserting that word or sentence as a truth of divine revelation.

For example, in Genesis 1:6 God says, "Let there be a firmament in the midst of the waters, and let it separate the waters from the waters." The word *firmament* comes from a Hebrew word that means "to be firmly hammered," and this "firmament" was thought to be a solid dome that held up waters above the earth. This is scientifically incorrect, of course, but it doesn't represent an error in Scripture because the author of Genesis wasn't trying to assert a geographical or cosmological truth.

Instead, the first two chapters of Genesis assert *theological* truths about God creating the world from nothing and making man in his image (which is also an anthropological truth). The language used to express these truths can reflect a variety of styles and literary approaches, and the Church acknowledges this. St. Thomas Aquinas, for example, said the *firmament* could refer to many kinds of celestial bodies and that "Moses was speaking to ignorant people, and that out of condescension to their weakness he put before them only such things as are apparent to sense."[43]

Most Protestants understand this, too. Jerry Walls, for example, says that Genesis does not teach a literal, six-day creation that occurred thousands of years ago because that interpretation contradicts "massive scientific evidence." Instead of being in error, the Bible must be asserting some other truth about God creating the world. But then, Walls claims Catholicism must be in error because the First Vatican Council teaches something about the papacy that seems to contradict the historical record:

> It was known in every age that the holy and most blessed Peter, prince and head of the apostles, the pillar of faith and the foundation of the Catholic Church, received the keys of the kingdom from our lord Jesus Christ, the Savior and redeemer of the human race, and that to this day and forever he lives and presides and exercises judgment in his successors the bishops of the holy Roman see, which he founded and consecrated with his blood (*Pastor Aeternus* 2).

This statement is false, say Walls and some other Protestant apologists, because early Christian witnesses disagree about the extent of the papal office. James White says, "Remember that Vatican I tells us that the Catholic Church has *always* [emphasis in the original] understood these passages, specifically Matthew 16 and John 21, in the way presented by Rome today. This is manifestly untrue."[44] Moreover, these critics point out that the early writings of the apostolic Fathers don't clearly articulate the grand claims of Vatican I in their description of the bishop of Rome.

But Protestants should give this statement in Vatican I the same flexibility they give to statements in Scripture that atheists claim are erroneous.

For example, Mark says John baptized "all the country of Judea, and all the people of Jerusalem" (1:5) even though John didn't baptize *every resident* of Jerusalem. When Jesus said the mustard seed is "the smallest of all the seeds on earth" (Mark 4:31), he was wrong from a strictly agricultural perspective, since there are smaller seeds. But it is a small seed, probably one of the smallest that local farmers knew about in the area. That means Jesus used an illustration that accommodated their limited knowledge and did not assert an erroneous scientific truth.

Similarly, the statement from Vatican I that these facts about the papacy were "known in every age" should be interpreted to refer to the knowledge of the papacy having an *apostolic origin*. This quotation from Vatican I comes from a representative (called a *legate*) of Pope Celestine I named Philip, who uttered it at the Council of Ephesus in 431. The fathers of Vatican I considered it fitting to include Philip's declaration in their decree defining papal infallibility since it is a very early witness to the doctrine of the papacy, even if the statement is not a strictly literal description of the knowledge of the papacy among every author in Church history.

This truth about the papacy was known during the time of the Church Fathers, even if it was not explicitly described in the earliest Fathers. To give a similar example, Protestants might say that the doctrine of the Trinity was known "in every age of Church history" even though the term was not used until the end of the second century and the doctrine was not clearly articulated until the beginning of the third century.[45] Or, they might say that true Christians "always understood and followed the Bible" even though, as we've seen, the first unambiguous witness to the canon of Scripture comes from the fourth century.

We should also consider that, unlike Sacred Scripture (all assertions of which are inerrant), statements of Church teaching are only guaranteed to be free from error when they involve infallible declarations of Christian truth. This happens in the solemn definitions of an ecumenical council or when the pope speaks *ex cathedra*. But the content of most magisterial statements in the Church's history are *not* such infallible declarations.[46]

This quotation from Vatican I about knowledge of Peter's successors being known "in every age" is not an infallible teaching. The only decree from that council that *is* infallible is the part that defines the conditions under which the pope is infallible; it begins by saying, "We teach and define as a divinely revealed dogma that . . ." The subsequent definition of papal infallibility does not make any historical claims about the papacy, and the prior language about the history of the papacy is not claimed to be inerrant.[47] And if it is fair for Protestants to distinguish what is written in Scripture from what is infallibly asserted in Scripture, then it is also fair for Catholics to make a similar distinction in the Church's magisterial teachings.

Some Protestants balk at this explanation, though, saying that restricting the Church's infallibility to only a few statements made under specific conditions empties the doctrine of any usefulness. Norm Geisler says, "Once all the qualifications are placed on infallibility, both in theory and in practice, it is defrocked of its glory."[48] But in his works defending the inerrancy of Scripture, Geisler says that doctrine only applies to the Bible's original autographs and so allows copyist errors to appear in later manuscripts. Geisler also says that inerrancy does not require the Bible to use scientific language, exact numbers, or even record the exact words Jesus or the apostles used on certain occasions.[49]

If these qualifications for biblical inerrancy don't "defrock" the Bible of its glory, then similar ones don't do the same for the Church's infallibility.

INFALLIBLE APOCRYPHA?

Another place that Protestant apologists look for "Catholic contradictions" that imitates secular skeptics is the deuterocanonical books of Scripture, which they call the *apocrypha*. These include seven books: 1 and 2 Maccabees, Tobit, Judith, Baruch, Wisdom, and Sirach, along with portions of Daniel and Esther. Protestants and modern Jews say they are not inspired; Catholics and Eastern Orthodox say they are. They were also found in the Septuagint—the Greek translation of the Old Testament that Jesus, the apostles, and the early Church Fathers used.

One argument made against these books is that they contain errors, and so they cannot be the inspired word of God. Evangelical scholar Josh McDowell says the deuterocanonical books "abound in historical and geographical inaccuracies and anachronisms. They teach doctrines which are false and foster practices which are at variance with inspired Scripture."[50] Ron Rhodes says that "historical and archaeological studies have always been the true friend of the canon of the Old and New Testaments, but they are clearly not the friend of apocryphal books."[51]

Of all the attempts to produce contradictions that undermine Catholicism, alleging errors in the deuterocanonical books is the feeblest. That's because it doesn't merely parallel arguments that atheists use against Scripture—it's the same argument. And that means Catholics can use the same replies that Protestants give to atheists when they attack Scripture.

Protestant apologists say we must remain convinced that because the Bible is the word of God, any *apparent* errors we find in it cannot be actual errors. Gleason Archer exhorts readers in his *Encyclopedia of Bible Difficulties* to "be fully persuaded in your own mind that an adequate explanation exists, even though you have not yet found it."[52] Norm Geisler and Thomas Howe give similar advice:

> No informed person would claim to be able to fully explain all Bible difficulties . . . the Christian scholar approaches the Bible with the same presumption that what

> is thus far unexplained is not therefore unexplainable. He or she does not assume that discrepancies are contradictions. And, when he encounters something for which he has no explanation, he simply continues to do research, believing that one will eventually be found.[53]

Notice that, for these Protestants, the presence or absence of error is not what determines if Scripture is inerrant. Rather, their belief that Scripture is the inspired word of God grounds the claim that Scripture *cannot possibly be* in error. This means that a Christian is justified in believing that the Bible is without error even if he can't explain every one of its apparent errors (which is true of nearly every Christian). The justification for Scripture's inerrancy flows from the Holy Spirit convincing him that the Bible is the word of God, and so he *knows* this "inerrant foundation" (i.e., divine inspiration) could never produce errors in the biblical text.

As we noted in chapter one, Protestants lack a consistent, objective means to determine which human writings are divinely inspired, so they lack a solid foundation to prove biblical inerrancy. Moreover, by using this approach Protestants can't falsify the deuterocanonical books of the Bible, since Catholics use this same approach to defend those books. Catholic apologist Gary Michuta writes,

> The determination of inspiration must necessarily come before any other question is asked. If a text is inspired, then all difficulties are understood to be errors only in appearance. If, on the other hand, one believes that a text is not inspired (i.e., it does not have the Holy Spirit as its primary author), then there is a possibility that the difficulty may be in fact a real error.[54]

In other words, we can't determine if any book is *divinely protected from error* until we first determine if it is *divinely inspired in its composition.* If it is inspired, then it is protected from error. Even if we can't explain every single alleged error in the Bible, those alleged errors do not constitute proof against its divine inspiration. Protestants employ this sequence of reasoning when defending the books of the Bible they affirm as Scripture against skeptical criticism, but then reverse it when attacking the deuterocanonical books of Scripture.

APPLYING INERRANCY TO THE DEUTEROCANON

With skeptics and Protestants alike, the alleged "difficulties" only arise because the critic reads the text in a rigid way that is designed to confirm his suspicion that it (the Bible/the deuterocanon) is full of errors.

In one debate I had on the deuterocanonical books, my opponent said the book of Tobit was in error because an angel tells Tobit to take the gall of a fish and "anoint with it a man who has white films in his eyes, and he will be cured" (Tob. 6:8), which Tobit later does to heal his blind father Tobias (11:7–8). "I would just like to ask Trent," said my opponent, "when's the last time that he put fish guts on his eyes for medicinal purposes."[55]

As I noted then in our debate, my opponent's dismissive attitude toward Tobit reminds me of atheists who ridicule Jesus' comments about the mustard seed (Mark 4:31) or Jacob's technique of having cattle mate in front of striped rods in order to produce striped offspring (Gen. 30–31). As I write in my book *Hard Sayings*, the latter case violates what we know about genetics—but in this story the Bible isn't asserting scientific truths about selective breeding (and later we learn that God was directly responsible for the improbable prospering of Jacob's cattle).[56]

Something similar may be said of the angel's reply in the book of Tobit. The text may also not be asserting anything about the medicinal use of fish balm. Jesus likewise wasn't prescribing a natural treatment for blindness when he put mud and spittle in the eyes of a blind man and told him to wash in the pool of Siloam (John 9:6–7). The healing of Tobias in Tobit 11 may be a similar miracle that used a natural element as a means to accomplish the healing.

On the other hand, it could also be the case that the ancient authors of Tobit knew more about medicine than we think. In the first century, the Roman natural scientist Pliny the Elder described using fish gall to treat eye problems, and a 1995 article in the *Journal of the Royal Society of Medicine* says the method described in Tobit may have been an ancient means of treating cataracts.[57] Granted, fish gall may not be as effective as modern medicine, but that doesn't mean the Bible erred in describing a popular ancient remedy.

Other Protestant critics claim that the book of Judith contains historical errors because it describes Nebuchadnezzar as the king of Assyria instead of as the king of Babylon (Jud. 1:1). But the protocanonical books have similar—if not more vexing—difficulties, like when Mark 2:26 says that David "entered the house of God, when Abiathar was high priest, and ate the bread of the Presence" even though 1 Samuel 21 says Abiathar's father *Ahimelech* was high priest when that happened, not Abiathar.[58] This is certainly an apparent error, but it is not apparent how it should be resolved.

The Protestant Greek scholar Daniel Wallace reviews a half-dozen different ways of explaining this difficulty, including that Jesus was not being literal in his description of who was high priest at that time in Israel's history.[59] Jesus could have referenced the more infamous Abiathar to make a point that the Pharisees would share his fate in being banished from Jerusalem for opposing God's chosen one, even though he wasn't technically high priest during the episode with David and the showbread.[60]

When it comes to Judith, both Catholic and Protestant scholars agree that non-literal language is being used and that the book's genre is closer to *didactic fiction* than historical chronicle. Since Judith means "Lady Jew," the story of her fighting a fanciful mishmash of Israel's enemies would be similar to an allegory about a woman named "Miss America" fighting Nazis being led by Joseph Stalin. One Protestant commenter observes that if the author of Judith read his work aloud, "he would have given his listeners a slight smile or a sly wink."[61]

WHEN CATHOLICS ARGUE LIKE ATHEISTS

If the Bible's divine authority can't be disproven through apparent errors, then this applies equally to the books found in Protestant *and* Catholic Bibles. But some Protestants may say in reply to this reasoning, "So what does Trent do when he examines the Quran or the Book of Mormon? Does he hesitate to say anything in those books is in error because he's afraid of 'arguing like an atheist'?"

Actually, I do.

Many of the alleged or apparent errors in these works have possible solutions, especially if the text is interpreted in a non-literal way. For example, it's easy to ridicule the Muslim belief that Muhammad split the moon in two while forgetting that the Bible says Joshua made the sun stand still for an entire day (Josh. 10:12–13).

Saying the Quran is false because it describes a globally observable miracle that lacks worldwide testimony exactly parallels atheists who make the same complaint about the biblical description of the sun standing still. In both cases, the critic leaps at the chance to falsify a holy text without investigating every avenue of defense for that text. But if the episode involving Joshua can be explained as a local, optical miracle that only the soldiers saw, or as a non-literal description of his success in battle, then similar explanations should be allowed for the Quran—or at least admitted as a possibility before further analysis.[62]

Of course, I think some aspects of non-Christian holy books are clearly in error, such as where they contradict what the Bible or the Church teaches. However, it takes effort to show how mere factual difficulties rise to a level of intractability that is not found in Bible difficulties.

Here's one example. Biblical events are geographically grounded. Christian, Jewish, and secular scholars generally agree where they roughly took place. Mormon scholars, on the other hand, have not reached any consensus about where the events described in the Book of Mormon took place. Their estimates have ranged from small portions of Central America, entire parts of North and South America, or small portions of the United States near the Great Lakes. This doesn't bode well for the book's historicity. It's no wonder that some liberal Mormon scholars say the Book of Mormon is not a literal history but an allegory meant to inspire faith.[63]

A better approach toward these books is to begin not with their apparent errors but the *foundational elements* of their distinct claims of inerrancy. For example, the primary reason I believe the Quran or the Book of Mormon is erroneous and uninspired is the lack of evidence for (as well as the presence of evidence against) their human authors having been the recipients of divine revelation. The reported testimony of

Muhammad or Joseph Smith is insufficient to convince me these books are divinely inspired.

I'm sure most Protestants become annoyed when atheists begin their investigation with the presumption that the Bible is erroneous and practically salivate at the prospect of tearing it apart. As one skeptic said of the book of Daniel, "Daniel may have survived meat-hungry lions, but fact-hungry historians have ripped him into shreds."[64] But the same thing can happen when a Protestant apologist sees the deuterocanon as something to "rip apart," even when its alleged errors are on par with or even less difficult than ones found in the protocanonical books.

So, if a Protestant were to make an argument against the deuterocanonical books of Scripture, it would be better for him to bypass claims of alleged error because this tactic can be easily weaponized against all the other books of the Bible. Instead, he should critically examine the authority that has declared these books are inspired and free from error, or the Magisterium of the Catholic Church.

4

PUSHING "PARALLELOMANIA"

In 1853, the Scottish Presbyterian theologian Alexander Hislop published a pamphlet entitled *The Two Babylons: Romanism and Its Origins* that was expanded into a book released after his death in 1903. Most of Hislop's arguments relied on supposed parallels showing that Catholicism was just an ancient Babylonian religion dressed up with Christian language. Fundamentalist authors in the late twentieth century took these arguments and put them into popular evangelism tracts.

The most popular of these, published by Jack Chick (known commonly as "Chick tracts"), contained stylized drawings depicting hapless Catholics appearing before God on judgment day, discovering they are damned because they belonged to a "pagan religion." Chick went on to publish tens of millions of tracts containing dubious assertions about the origins of Catholic practices. These include the claim that the Eucharist comes from ancient Egypt and that it was the Babylonian king Nimrod who "came up with the idea of confessionals and celibacy for the priesthood."[65]

Protestants who are sympathetic to Hislop's basic argument (even if they don't endorse all of his conclusions) should be careful, since Hislop also criticizes practices that most Protestants consider innocuous. For example, he condemns the celebration of Easter as a carryover from paganism, claiming that the name of the holiday "bears its Chaldean origin on its very forehead. Easter is nothing else than Astarte, one of the titles of Beltis, the queen of heaven."[66]

In fact, modern atheists make similar arguments when they claim that Easter is a celebration of the pagan god Ishtar.[67] And when we look at how Protestants respond to these atheistic "pagan parallel" arguments, we see those responses just as easily answer Fundamentalist "pagan parallel" arguments against Catholicism.

ARE CHRISTIANS THE REAL PAGANS?

Atheists who believe that Jesus never existed (called *mythicists*) claim there are damning parallels between the story of Jesus and stories of other "dying and rising" gods. But instead of reading about this in a pamphlet like Hislop's, you're more likely to come across mythicist arguments through online videos such as *Zeitgeist*, which claims:

- the Egyptian god Horus "was born on December 25 of the virgin Isis-Meri . . . at the age of thirty he was baptized by a figure known as Anup and thus began his ministry. Horus had twelve disciples he traveled about with, performing miracles such as healing the sick and walking on water . . . Horus was crucified, buried for three days, and thus, resurrected";
- the Greek god Dionysus was "born of a virgin on December

25, was a traveling teacher who performed miracles such as turning water into wine." *Zeitgeist* also claims that the Roman god Mithra was born of a virgin on December 25;

- ancient pagan cults also worshipped the "Sun" by mourning when it died in the winter and celebrating when it "rises" in the spring to bring forth new crops.

Although similarity between beliefs can be evidence that one culture was the source for another culture's belief, in many other instances it can lead to a bad case of "parallelomania." Biblical scholar Samuel Sandmel says this happens when a person falsely believes cultural borrowing has taken place and tries to prove it with highly implausible parallels. Straining to make connections, the "parallelomaniac" ignores more plausible explanations for why two different religions might have similar beliefs, stories, traditions, or customs.

For instance, in some cases, the imagined parallel simply doesn't exist at all. In others, the alleged parallels are so trivial that they don't really serve as evidence for culture-borrowing. Or it might, on closer inspection, turn out that the borrowing happened the other way around (e.g., paganism borrowing from Christianity). Or the borrowing might be real but related only to non-essential areas of belief.

When we apply these alternative explanations, we see that neither Catholicism nor Christianity can be explained as mere offshoots of older pagan practices. Let's start with the first explanation—when parallels never existed in the first place.

"MYTHING" IN ACTION

Many of *Zeitgeist's* claims about ancient non-Christian religions simply aren't true. There is no evidence the Egyptian god Horus was baptized, had twelve disciples, performed miracles like walking on water, or that he was crucified. In at least one instance, a deity that is supposed to parallel Jesus turns out to have never existed in pagan mythology. *Zeitgeist* claims that "Beddru" of Japan and "Crite" of Chaldea inspired the Jesus story, but there is no record of any deities by these names having a cult of worship.

Why would the producers of this film, or other mythicists, make up stuff like this? Odds are, they acted in good faith but uncritically followed older, amateur scholarship that had a bad habit of using poorly documented sources.

Many of their claims about Horus, for example, come straight from self-anointed (and long discredited) scholars from the nineteenth century, such as Gerald Massey. Contemporary Egyptologists do not trust his work today, and even Massey's peers rejected his scholarship. The renowned British Museum Egyptologist Archibald Sayce, for instance, commended an 1888 article for its "through demolition of Mr. Massey's crudities [and] errors." His colleague Peter le Page Renouf said of Massey that "no lunatic could possibly write more wild rubbish."[68]

When we turn to anti-Catholicism, we see similar uncritical reliance on Hislop's shoddy scholarship. This is evident in claims from Chick tracts such as, "The Holy Eucharist is placed in the center of a sunburst design called the monstrance. . . . Who dreamed this up? The Egyptians called it Osiris long before the popes called it Jesus."[69] Sure enough, Gerald Massey claimed that, in Egyptian worship, "flesh and beer were transelemented or transubstantiated by the descent of Ra the holy spirit" and that this sacrament was "continued by the Church of Rome."[70]

Chick further claims that the eucharistic host has the monogram *IHS* on it because in Egypt these letters stood for the gods Isis, Horus, and Seb. However, there is no evidence that ancient Egyptian religion had anything like the Eucharist, much less a host that included a monogram with the Latin letters IHS. (In reality, these three letters are often found on eucharistic hosts because they are derived from the first three letters of Jesus' name in Greek.)

Because of these blunders even some of Hislop's defenders came to realize that his thesis was indefensible. One of these people was Protestant author Ralph Woodrow, who adapted Hislop's research and published it in 1966 in the (much more readable) *Babylon Mystery Religion*. Several decades later, though, Woodrow realized that the evidence did not support Hislop's claims and, in many cases, even contradicted them. This led to the publication of Woodrow's 1997 book *The Babylon Connection?* where he denounced his previous book and took Hislop to task for several egregious historical fictions.

These fictions included the claim that Nimrod and Semiramis were married Babylonian royalty who created a "proto-pagan-Catholicism." This isn't possible, since, as modern scholars agree, they didn't even live during the same period. Other claims, like "Catholic confessionals have a Babylonian origin," ignore the historical reality that the Church practiced the sacrament of confession *without confessionals* for centuries. The regular practice of confessing privately to a priest in a reserved place was introduced into the Church through Irish missionaries in the early Middle Ages, not a Babylonian cult in late antiquity.[71]

SKIN-DEEP SIMILARITIES

In many cases, the alleged parallel between Christianity and paganism only exists in the creative mind of the parallelomaniac. In some other cases, though, the evidence from primary sources is accurate—and so a genuine parallel does exist—but the parallel is so trivial or general that it says nothing about any cultural borrowing. Ancient pagan deities, for example, may have performed miracles just as Jesus did, but we'd expect that *any* story about deities interacting with human beings would include miraculous details.[72] So those similarities don't suggest any borrowing.

Other alleged parallels are true only if you really strain your eyes and your reading comprehension. For example, mythicists say the Persian deity Mithra was born of a virgin (just like Jesus!) but the ancient source actually says that Mithra *emerged fully-grown from a rock*.[73] This is only a "virgin birth" in the most contorted sense of that term.

Similarly, that *sun* and *son* are homophones is true in English but not most other languages, including ancient languages like Greek or Hebrew. A similar error occurs in the identification of Easter with *Ishtar* (and honestly, the two sound similar only if you are prone to slurring your speech). Even more fatal to this alleged parallel is that nearly all European languages call the celebration of Christ's resurrection a variant of the Latin word *pascha*. Christ is our new Passover (or *paschal*) lamb, as St. Paul describes him in 1 Corinthians 5:7. (*Easter* comes from older Germanic words signifying springtime and the dawn.)

Modern scholarship has also shown that Christian and Catholic beliefs are primarily rooted in Judaism, not paganism. In his study on ancient resurrection belief, T.N.D. Mettinger put it this way:

> There is, as far as I am aware, no *prima facie* evidence that the death and resurrection of Jesus is a mythological construct, drawing on myths and rites of the dying and rising gods of the surrounding world. While studied with

> profit against the background of Jewish resurrection belief, the faith in the death and resurrection of Jesus retains its unique character in the history of religions.[74]

And the same is true of Catholic practices that some Protestants falsely decry as being examples of pagan infiltration into the Church.

For example, Hislop (and many other Protestants) see Catholic veneration of Mary as a carryover of ancient pagan goddess worship. But in the Old Testament, King Solomon's mother Bathsheba was called the "great lady" in Hebrew (a similar title in English, found in the British monarchy, would be *queen mother*). This Great Lady sat at the king's right hand and wore a crown, and people even sought her intercession with the king (1 Kings 2:20). There is no need to go looking in paganism for a forerunner or type of Mary—it's right in Scripture.

It's true that in the pagan world many goddesses were considered the "queen of heaven," and it is wrong to worship them, but that doesn't make it wrong to appropriately honor the true Queen of Heaven. The Bible refers to pagan rulers like Artaxerxes (Ezra 7:12) and Nebuchadrez'zar (Ez. 26:7) as "king of kings" but this wouldn't make Jesus' title "king of kings" (Rev. 17:14) a pagan one or make it wrong to call him by that title.

In any case, the existence of counterfeit deities does not count against worship of the true king or veneration of the true king's mother. Similarly, if Catholic art depicting Mary holding the infant Jesus is wrong because it superficially resembles pagan duos like Isis and her son Horus, then Christian art depicting Jesus with a halo or wearing white would be wrong because those works superficially resemble art depicting pagan gods like Apollo.

While we're on the subject of art: one Protestant website warns its readers, "The next time you are in a Catholic church, take a look around. What do you see? Statues? Candles? A priest shaking the incense burner? . . . People, doing all that is a sin!"[75] Yet the Old Testament describes statues being created for the purpose of healing people (Num. 25:8) and censers being used to spread incense for worship because the smoke symbolizes our prayers rising up to God (Lev. 16:12–13). The fact that pagans used candles and incense doesn't mean that the Old Testament "borrowed" this worship from paganism.

It's reasonable to expect human beings in different eras and cultures to exhibit similar religious tendencies, because it's in our nature. God created us to be religious. The *Catechism* puts it this way:

> In many ways, throughout history down to the present day, men have given expression to their quest for God in their religious beliefs and behavior: in their prayers, sacrifices, rituals, meditations, and so forth. These forms of religious expression, despite the ambiguities they often bring with them, are so universal that one may well call man a religious being (28).

Indeed, Woodrow also saw how the parallelomania he embraced earlier in his career could be repurposed against Christianity as a whole:

> As Christians, we don't reject prayer just because pagans pray to their gods. We don't reject water baptism just because ancient tribes plunged into water as a religious ritual. We don't reject the Bible just because pagans believe their writings are holy or sacred . . . If finding

> a pagan parallel provides proof of paganism, the Lord himself would be pagan.[76]

PRAISEWORTHY PAGAN PARALLELS

Some Catholic practices do genuinely parallel pagan practices, but this was consciously done in order to take something good in pagan culture and "baptize" it for use in Christian worship. Pope St. John Paul II said, "Through inculturation the Church makes the gospel incarnate in different cultures . . . It transmits to them its own values, at the same time taking the good elements that already exist in them and renewing them from within."[77] One example of this inculturation is the Pantheon in Rome, which was once a temple that contained statues of all the ancient gods but was consecrated to St. Mary and the martyrs in 609.

However, this "lingering paganism" is still a cause for concern for Protestants like Jimmy Swaggart, who said,

> An overwhelming percentage of the rites and ceremonies of the Roman Catholic Church are of pagan origin. Cardinal Newman, in his book, *The Development of the Christian Doctrine* ([a] Catholic), admits that "temples, incense, oil lamps, votive offerings, holy water, holidays and seasons of devotions, processions, blessing of fields, sacerdotal vestments, the tonsure [of priests, monks, and nuns], and images . . . are all of pagan origin."[78]

Swaggart fails to mention, or to realize, that Protestants have also borrowed elements from paganism that complement rather than contradict their faith. Two examples can be found in Newman's original writing that Swaggart fails to include in the previous quotation. In that excerpt, Newman speaks of "the use of calendars" and giving "the ring in marriage"—things Protestants do and have no problem with—as pagan practices that Catholics adopted.

Another example would be church buildings themselves. Early Christians worshipped in private homes, not set-apart buildings. The very first author to use the phrase "go to church" was Clement of Alexandria—in the third century.[79] The idea of a building whose sole purpose was for communal worship (as opposed to a home that doubled as a place of worship) was not known in Christianity until the fourth century. Of course, pagans had been using them for centuries.

But so what? Even in the natural religious impulses of pagans, God was preparing humanity for his revelation and for true worship. The nineteenth-century Protestant historian Philip Schaff noted that "there lurked in those pagan festivals themselves, in spite of all their sensual abuses, a deep meaning and an adaptation to a real want; they might be called unconscious prophecies of the Christmas feast."[80]

C.S. Lewis reached a similar conclusion when he said that God had revealed himself indirectly to pagans through their myths and that the Gospels were now God's direct revelation. They were, as he said, "myth become fact." I'll close with his advice that shows that Catholics and Christians have nothing to fear from "pagan parallels": "We must not be nervous about 'parallels' and 'pagan Christs': they ought to be there—it would be a stumbling block if they weren't. We must not, in false spirituality, withhold our imaginative welcome."[81]

WHEN CATHOLICS ARGUE LIKE ATHEISTS

So far, we've seen that some Protestants accuse Catholicism of being a warmed-over version of paganism. In return, sometimes Catholics claim that Protestantism is just a new form of the old Gnostic heresies from the first few centuries of Church history.

Gnostics emphasized a secret knowledge of salvation and a preference for the spiritual over the material. Some modern Protestants say that Christianity isn't a religion but a "relationship," and so salvation is about knowing God personally through faith. Protestants also have an aversion to mediated or material means of encountering God, such as sacraments (especially the Mass), sacramentals, and venerating icons and relics.

So, on the one hand, it isn't entirely unfair to compare Protestantism to Gnosticism. Calvinist author Michael Horton says that "critics of modern American religion are basically on target in describing the entire religious landscape, from New Age or liberal, to evangelical and Pentecostal, as essentially Gnostic."[82] The Protestant author Philip Lee even wrote a whole book on the subject in 1987 called *Against the Protestant Gnostics*. Lee pointed out that Protestants do have a tendency of spiritualizing and subjectivizing Christianity in a way that downplays its material and corporal elements.

There are parallels between Protestantism and Gnosticism—just as there are parallels between Catholicism and paganism. But Catholics argue like atheists when they try to compartmentalize all of Protestantism under the Gnostic label. It may be the case that some Protestants have, perhaps unintentionally, fallen into the same thinking as Gnostics. But this wouldn't mean that Protestantism itself is Gnostic in nature or to the root—only that it needs to be purified of these disordered ways of thinking.

One feature of ancient paganism was mindless ritualism. Our Lord even warned his audience to "not heap up empty phrases as the Gentiles [i.e., pagans] do; for they think that they will be heard for their many words" (Matt. 6:7). Yet some Catholics do end up unintentionally treating the rosary as an incantation to be uttered instead of as a set of mysteries for spiritual meditation. In some cultures, Catholics do treat statues and images in a way that overstates their intrinsic power, as pagans treated idols. But neither of these things proves that Catholicism is pagan. It only proves that human tendencies can infect any kind of godly worship.

Just as Catholics are nothing like pagans in many important ways, so too do Protestants differ from Gnostics in important ways. Unlike the Gnostics, who disparaged marriage and prized celibacy, Protestants insist upon marriage too much and value celibacy not enough. The Gnostics restricted salvation to hidden knowledge that was given only to the properly initiated, whereas Protestants have historically worked to make the Gospel as publicly accessible as possible through things like tracts, hotel room Bibles, and open-air revivals.

So, although it may be valid to point out where Protestants or Catholics have inadvertently fallen into "bad pagan habits," it's not valid to cite superficial "pagan parallels" as the primary way to discredit an entire belief system.

5

ARGUMENTS FROM SILENCE

Sometimes, Protestant apologists will admit that certain Catholic doctrines are well attested in the writings of the Church Fathers, even though they think the doctrines are not taught in the Bible. William Webster rejects baptismal regeneration as unbiblical, for example, but he acknowledges that "the doctrine of baptism is one of the few teachings within Roman Catholicism for which it can be said that there is a universal consent of the Fathers."[83] Norm Geisler and Ralph Mackenzie admit that the early Church believed that the apostles' teaching authority was preserved through successors (*apostolic succession*), but downplay this fact by claiming that "simply because a teaching existed early in church history that does not make it true."[84]

According to these same apologists though, the *absence* of other Catholic doctrines in the writings of the Church Fathers proves those doctrines are false! One common example they cite is the bodily assumption of Mary into heaven. Webster says, "For centuries in the early Church there is complete silence regarding Mary's end," and Geisler and Mackenzie claim the belief was "not held by most of the early church fathers."[85]

These apologists are making "arguments from silence" against Catholicism. They say, "If Catholicism were true, then doctrine X would be described in the writings of certain Church Fathers. But doctrine X is not found among certain Church Fathers. Therefore, Catholicism is false." In doing so, they are arguing like atheists. For if you swap out *Catholicism* for *Christianity*, you can find identical arguments from silence claiming that major Christian doctrines must be unbiblical novelties because they are conspicuously absent from early Christian sources.

This doesn't mean that Catholics and Protestants should never use arguments from silence. They can be valid, but we must be careful in defining when a mere "lack of evidence" becomes a "deafening silence" that casts serious doubt upon a belief. When Protestants set the bar too low in critiques of Catholic doctrines, they risk having to tolerate non-Christians using the same measure in their critiques of fundamental Christian doctrines.

UNDERSTANDING "ARGUMENTS FROM SILENCE"

One example of an argument from silence against Christian doctrine comes from early twentieth-century liberal Protestants who doubted the historicity of the virgin birth. One of them, Harry Emerson Fosdick, declared in a sermon entitled "Shall the Fundamentalists Win?" that "the two men who contributed most to the Church's thought of the divine meaning of the Christ were Paul and John, who never even distantly allude to the virgin birth."[86] The arguments can still be found among modern critical scholars such as Bart

Ehrman, who says that in Mark's Gospel "there is no word of Jesus' pre-existence or of his birth to a virgin. Surely if this author believed in either view, he would have mentioned it."[87]

Arguments from silence are also popular among mythicists who say that Jesus never existed as a human being. They claim that the first Christians instead thought of Jesus as a "cosmic savior" figure who appeared in visions to them. Richard Carrier makes this point by citing the lack of details about Jesus' earthly ministry in Paul's writings:

> Never once is his baptism mentioned, or his ministry, or his trial, or any of his miracles, or any historical details about what he was like, what he did, or suffered, or where he was from, or where he had been, or what people he knew. No memories from those who knew him are ever reported. Paul never mentions Galilee or Nazareth, or Pilate or Mary or Joseph, or any miracles Jesus did or any miraculous powers he is supposed to have displayed.[88]

Remember that not all arguments from silence are faulty. One argument for an early date of the Acts of the Apostles thus rests on the fact that Acts does not record events like the deaths of Peter and Paul or the destruction of the Temple in Jerusalem. These things aren't *proof* that Acts was written early, but it does make it more likely given that it would have been odd for a historian like Luke to omit such important events in his account of the apostolic Church.

The key to making a successful argument from silence, though, lies in being able to show that if an event actually happened, it is *highly likely* an author would have written about it—and so his silence on the matter is evidence it didn't happen. The argument can't rest on it merely being *possible* or even *fitting* for an author to have written about a certain topic.

For example, historians agree that Marco Polo went to China even though he never mentions the Great Wall of China in his travel diaries. The first-century Jewish historian Josephus never mentions the writings of Paul, even though Paul was a Pharisee who became one of Christianity's leading theologians, and so would have been infamous.[89] Of course, these cases don't show that Paul's conversion or the Great Wall of China are myths.

This is why the Protestant scholar Timothy McGrew says, "It is a risky business to speculate upon the motives of authors for including or omitting various facts."[90] In another essay, McGrew provides a litany of strange historical silences, including Ulysses Grant's omission of the Emancipation Proclamation in his recounting of the Civil War. McGrew then asks, "At what point is it unreasonable for us, in the face of an avalanche of such examples, to retain our initial confidence regarding what ancient authors *would* have said?"[91]

It's no wonder that, as the early twentieth-century Protestant theologian Charles Briggs said in reply to liberal scholars who used these arguments against the virgin birth, that "the argument from silence cannot be used as a nose of wax to prove anything you please."[92]

ANSWERING ARGUMENTS FROM SILENCE

One way to answer arguments from silence is to show they prove too much. In 1924, J. Gresham Machen pointed out how liberal Christians were being inconsistent in denying the virgin birth simply because Paul did not explicitly teach the doctrine. He noted that "the center of their religion is found in the ethical teaching of Jesus, especially in the Golden Rule. But where does Paul say anything about the Golden Rule, and where does he quote at any length the ethical teachings of Jesus?"[93]

The same reply can be given to mythicists who crow about the dozens of ancient, non-Christian historians who never mention Jesus Christ. Those same sources also don't mention the existence of *Christians*, but no one offers this as proof that Christians did not exist in the first century. The silence in these sources about Christ and Christians only proves that these pagan historians were either unaware of Jesus and his followers or that they had little concern for what they probably considered to be myths or idle tales (see 2 Pet. 1:16).

That arguments from silence can prove too much is evident in arguments that Protestants make against the existence of a bishop of Rome in the first century. Protestant apologists say that because Ignatius of Antioch (A.D. 110) did not name the bishop of Rome or greet him in his letter to the Romans, such a person did not exist. Yet Ignatius also doesn't mention priests, deacons, or even any lay faithful by name in his letter to the Roman church; but that wouldn't prove there were no Christians in Rome!

What's more likely is that Ignatius, who is on his way to Rome to be executed, deliberately omits details about the Roman Christians in order to protect them from imperial persecution. In his other letters, Ignatius makes it clear that that a local church is only valid if it has a bishop presiding over it, and so his effusive praise for the church at Rome wouldn't make sense if it lacked something that was necessary for it to be a valid church in the first place.[94] And indeed, later sources—such as St. Irenaeus, who wrote just a few decades later—confirm that there were bishops in Rome in the first century.[95]

Another way to answer arguments from silence is to show that the silence isn't scandalous. For example, it's true that Paul does not mention many aspects of Christ's earthly ministry. Neither do the sermons in the book of Acts. However, the author of Acts was clearly aware of Christ's earthly ministry, since he wrote the Gospel of Luke! Early Christians thought that Jesus' earthly ministry was important, but not every source chose to write about it directly. This also includes first-century Fathers like St. Clement of Rome, who allude to the Gospels but don't talk about specific elements of Jesus' earthly ministry.

The Protestant scholar Michael Kruger points out that the apparent silences in some early Christian sources may not be intentional but may be a result of texts being lost over the centuries. The Fathers certainly weren't immune to this, as can be seen in works like Papias's five-volume *Exposition on the Logia of the Lord*. It was written in the second century but currently exists only as a few fragments that were cited by other authors. In this vein, Kruger gives another example from the New Testament that shows how arguments from silence can lead to rash conclusions:

> Think, for example, of Paul's discussion of Jesus instituting the Lord's Supper in 1 Corinthians 11:23–26—a topic he never discusses anywhere else. Now, imagine for a moment that (for some reason), we didn't have 1 Corinthians. We might conclude that Paul didn't know about Jesus instituting the Lord's Supper; indeed, we might even conclude that Paul didn't believe in the institution of the Lord's Supper. And we would be flat out wrong.[96]

ARGUMENTS FROM SILENCE AGAINST PROTESTANTISM?

A Protestant might reply to skeptics that although the absence of details about Jesus' life in Paul or Clement may be odd, it is not a fatal objection to Christianity. We still have the canonical

Gospels to tell us about Jesus' earthly life and ministry. The silence in these cases relates merely to the question of why one source reports a fact whereas another one doesn't. But, they might say in turn to Catholics, when it comes to dogmas like the assumption of Mary, *no source* explicitly mentions it for several centuries after the birth of Christ.

Even this modified standard for an argument from silence, however, can be used against important Christian doctrines.

No Church Fathers mention anything approaching a New Testament canon of Scripture until Irenaeus at the end of the second century, and his canon doesn't match the one we have today. As I noted earlier, the first complete description of the New Testament canon is not found in any source until the late fourth century. What spurred the Fathers to write on this subject were the second-century Marcionite heretics who rejected several inspired books. According to Protestant scholar F.F. Bruce, "In the Marcionite controversy an answer had to be given to the more fundamental question: what is the Bible? . . . If they had not given much thought to the limits of holy writ previously, they had to pay serious attention to the question now."[97]

Baptist theologian Matthew Emerson cautions his fellow Protestants against reading too much into the silence of the Fathers on a given subject, since they often focused on certain theological topics to the neglect of others. When we don't take this into account, he says, "historically, this 'argument from patristic (or medieval) silence' is an error of anachronism."[98]

Another reason to take Emerson's caution seriously is that some Protestant doctrines are absent, not just from the early Church, but from nearly all of pre-Reformation history. When it comes to justification by faith alone, for instance, Geisler and Mackenzie admit that "between the time of the apostle Paul and the Reformation, scarcely anyone taught imputed righteousness, or forensic justification."[99] Another example is the doctrine of eternal security, which claims that a Christian cannot lose his salvation. Even Calvinist theologians who affirm this doctrine do not locate it prior to the sixteenth century.[100]

Some Protestants might be willing to grant that the pre-Reformation Church did not teach important doctrines like forensic justification or eternal security. But since they believe in *sola scriptura*, the only thing that matters is whether *the Bible* teaches these doctrines—not whether any Church Fathers or anyone else in Christian history taught them. Emerson puts it this way:

> For Protestants, the ultimate doctrinal standard is not a particular period in church history or how early or late a particular doctrine is widely attested, but whether or not a particular doctrine is faithful to Holy Scripture. While we certainly want to pay attention to any belief's development, our assessment of it, if we are to be fully Protestant, should rest finally with whether or not it conforms to God's Word.[101]

Now, this is a consistent position for a Protestant who only looks to the Fathers for theological reflection and doesn't use their omissions as proofs in polemics against Catholicism. But holding Emerson's attitude while also using the Fathers to disprove Catholic doctrine amounts to a game of "heads I win, tails you lose."

Most Protestant arguments from silence in relation to the Fathers seem to assume as a premise that if a doctrine were apostolic in origin (like the assumption of Mary), then we'd expect the early Fathers to have mentioned it. But if that claim were true, wouldn't it prove that Protestant doctrines like eternal security or the denial of baptismal regeneration are not apostolic because the Fathers either didn't mention them or even universally taught against them?

A Protestant might say in response that because those doctrines can be found in Scripture, they are apostolic even if they aren't explicit in the Fathers. But are they found in Scripture, or are they found in certain *interpretations* of Scripture? If these major doctrines about how salvation is gained or lost were in Scripture, then it would be highly unusual for the majority (or in some cases the entirety) of pre-Reformation Christians to fail to notice them.

WHEN CATHOLICS ARGUE LIKE ATHEISTS

Obviously more could be said about which arguments from silence in relation to ancient doctrine are plausible and which are flimsy. The key for us is not to use arguments from silence indiscriminately. Our Lord's advice in the Sermon on the Mount applies in this case: the measure you give will be the measure you get (Matt. 7:2). That's why I've stopped using certain arguments from silence against Protestantism, or at least rhetorical flourishes that have the same purpose.

For example, in the past I've asked Protestants, "Which Church Father would you be comfortable having as a pastor in your Church?" or "Which Church Father holds to your theology?" The goal of the questions was to make an implicit argument from silence to show that Protestantism is unhistorical and thus not apostolic in origin. But I've since realized that these questions aren't helpful because they can be turned against Catholics.

For example, I would love to have St. Thomas Aquinas as a pastor at my church, but he denied the traditional teaching on the Immaculate Conception. This doesn't show that Aquinas wasn't Catholic, since that doctrine would not be formally defined for another 600 years. But it does show that one can claim a saint or Father as a "spiritual ancestor" even if they don't share every facet of one's current theology.

If we allow for Catholic doctrine to have developed over time and still to have maintained continuity with the apostles, then we should be courteous to Protestants who attempt a similar explanation for the presence of their beliefs in Church history.

6

CONSTANT[INE] CONSPIRACY THEORIES

One common argument against Catholicism is that it began not with Jesus and the apostles but in the fourth century, under the newly converted Roman emperor Constantine. According to this theory, after Christianity went from being a persecuted minority to a tolerated (and later official) religion of the Roman Empire, pagan converts entered the Church in order to improve their social status. In doing so, they brought their pagan ideas into the Church and corrupted its pure, apostolic message—creating Roman Catholicism.[102]

Some secular scholars take this argument one step further. They claim that Constantine was responsible not just for distinctly Catholic theology, but for all Christian theology. Religious studies professor Paul Flesher claims that in the fourth century "there was little agreement about Christianity's beliefs and teachings, the nature of Jesus and God, what writings were sacred, or even how to worship."[103]

According to critics like Flesher, Constantine became the person who created unity among Christians by mandating belief in the divinity of Christ and deciding which books belonged in the Bible. This theory even appears in popular works like *The Da Vinci Code* where one character, a historian named Teabing, makes the bold claim that "Jesus' establishment as 'the Son of God' was officially proposed and voted on by the Council of Nicaea" and that it was a "relatively close" vote.[104]

When *The Da Vinci Code* was released in 2003, it prompted a flurry of responses from Christians (and even some agnostic scholars, such as Bart Ehrman) who took the book to task for its revisionist view of Christian history. Given the liberties Brown took with historical facts related to Jesus and Catholicism, these critics also noted the audacity of a claim in the book's preface that states: "All descriptions of artwork, architecture, documents, and secret rituals in this novel are accurate."

In this very close example of Protestants arguing like atheists, critical responses to books like *The Da Vinci Code* help to answer not only the claim that "Constantine invented Christianity" but the common Protestant claim that "Constantine invented Catholicism" as well.

CRACKING THE *CODE*

The Da Vinci Code (and other books, scholars, internet memes, etc. that continue to make the same kind of claims today) makes it seem like, by the time of the Council of Nicaea in A.D. 325, Christians weren't even sure if Jesus was

God, and so the matter came down to a nail-biting vote. But as Bart Ehrman notes, "There certainly was no vote to determine Jesus' divinity: this was already a matter of common knowledge among Christians, and had been from the early years of the religion."[105]

At Nicaea, the bishops were voting on how Jesus' divinity should be *understood and expressed*, not on whether it was an object of Christian belief. They asked, "Was Jesus equal in divinity with the Father or just similar in divinity to the Father?" The result of the final vote yielded 316 bishops in favor of Jesus being equal in divinity with the Father and none in favor of the view he is only similar to the Father (two bishops abstained from voting). The vote at Nicaea was indeed "relatively close"—to being a unanimous affirmation of the orthodox Catholic faith.

Other Protestant critics of *The Da Vinci Code* point out that belief in Jesus' divinity long preceded the time of Emperor Constantine. In the second century, Ignatius of Antioch called Jesus "our God" and the Greek Father Aristides said, "God came down from heaven, and from a Hebrew virgin assumed and clothed himself with flesh."[106] This is also attested in *non-Christian* sources, such as the playwright Lucian of Samosata, who ridiculed Christians for "denying the Greek gods, and by worshipping that crucified sophist himself and living according to his laws."[107] Pliny the Younger describes Christians singing a hymn to Christ "as to a God" and an early third-century drawing called the *Alexamanos graffito* shows a Roman soldier worshipping a man with a donkey head being crucified. The drawing's caption reads, "Alexamanos worship [your] God."[108]

The Da Vinci Code also claims that Constantine invented widespread disciplines in the Church, such as priestly celibacy and worshipping on Sunday. And some Protestants who loathe these disciplines think a "Constantine conspiracy" is a good way to make their case. According to former nun Mary Ann Collins, "The fact that Constantine saw the cross and the sun together may explain why he worshipped the Roman sun god while at the same time professing to be a Christian . . . Constantine made Sunday (the day of the sun god) into a day of rest when work was forbidden."[109]

But in his book *The Da Vinci Code: A Quest for Answers*, Protestant author Josh McDowell replies to the claim that Constantine initiated Sunday worship to coincide with pagan veneration of the sun. He points out that Constantine "is about 250 years late," and he cites the New Testament as well as the writings of Justin Martyr to show that Christians worshipped on Sunday—and not to serve the "sun god."[110]

THE ANCIENT, CATHOLIC FAITH

When we look at this same historical evidence, we see that it is not only traditional Christian doctrines and practices that predated Constantine—it is Catholic ones, as well. There have been many books written on the evidence for Catholic doctrines in the early Church, so we won't survey all the evidence these excellent works have already covered.[111] I'll just point out where sources that both Protestants and Catholics use to defend the antiquity of Christian beliefs (like the divinity of Christ) also attest to the antiquity of Catholic beliefs (for example, the real presence of Christ in the Eucharist), thus making it impossible for the latter to have been a product of Constantine's influence.

Ignatius of Antioch not only believed that it was heretical to deny the divinity of Christ, but also that those who "confess not the Eucharist to be the flesh of our Savior Jesus Christ, which suffered for our sins, and which the Father, of his goodness, raised up again" are heretics.[112] Justin Martyr said that the eucharistic prayer at Mass changes the bread and wine so it becomes "the flesh and blood of that Jesus who was made flesh."[113] Belief in the Real Presence was so strong that Christians were often accused of cannibalism, a charge Justin refutes in his *Apology* to the Roman emperor. Pliny the Younger wrote in his report to Emperor Trajan that Christians "partake of food—but ordinary and innocent food," which implies that he was aware of accusations that Christians partook in extraordinary and "guilty" food, like the flesh of human beings.[114]

It's understandable that pagan outsiders would misunderstand the Eucharist, because Christians used not only vivid language of eating flesh (as the Lord himself used in John 6:53–57) but considered the Eucharist to be the perfect *sacrifice*: a re-presentation of the one sacrifice Christ had made on the cross, though under the form of bread and wine. The evidence flatly contradicts Protestant authors such as Frank Viola and George Barnes, who claim that "when Roman Catholicism evolved in the fourth to the sixth centuries, it absorbed many of the religious practices of both paganism and Judaism. It set up a professional priesthood. It erected sacred buildings. And it turned the Lord's Supper into a mysterious sacrifice."[115]

The early Church did not borrow its eucharistic theology from pagan notions of temple sacrifice or even from Judaism (which existed without priests or sacrifices since the destruction of the temple in A.D. 70). Instead, the Church saw the Eucharist as the fulfillment of the one true sacrifice, in Christ, that was prophesied in the Old Testament. Justin Martyr and Irenaeus both saw the Eucharist as the fulfillment of the prophecy of Malachi 1:11: "In every place incense is offered to my name, and a pure offering; for my name is great among the nations, says the LORD of hosts."[116] In the third century, St. Cyprian wrote of "professional priests" to whom people confessed their sins and through whom Christ's eternal priesthood was imitated:

> For if Jesus Christ, our Lord and God, is himself the chief priest of God the Father, and has first offered himself a sacrifice to the Father, and has commanded this to be done in commemoration of himself, certainly that priest truly discharges the office of Christ, who imitates that which Christ did; and he then offers a true and full sacrifice in the Church to God the Father, when he proceeds to offer it according to what he sees Christ himself to have offered.[117]

Even Protestant apologists who deny that the Mass and the priesthood have apostolic origins recognize that these elements of the Catholic faith long predate Constantine. William Webster, for example, admits that Cyprian believed in the third century that the Mass was a propitiatory sacrifice (one that takes away sin), though he explains it away as part of an early shift into heresy, claiming that was only because "the Church at this time was drifting from reliance on God's grace in Jesus Christ to a theology which included the concept of human works."[118]

All of this shows that the Roman emperor Constantine invented neither Catholicism nor Christianity, since the important doctrines of these theological systems predated him—sometimes by several hundred years. Moreover, if Protestants claim that Constantine fabricated the antiquity of the Catholic faith, then they undermine their own arguments against the impossibility of his inventing a brand-new form of Christianity.

For example, the Protestant apologist Greg Koukl scoffs at the theory that Constantine destroyed the earlier Gospels that depicted a merely human Jesus and replaced them with what we now call the canonical Gospels. Koukl writes of the apocryphal gospels, "How is it physically possible for Constantine to gather up all of the handwritten copies from every nook and cranny of the Roman Empire by the fourth century and destroy the vast majority of them?"[119]

Koukl is correct. If it took the United States a decade with technology like military satellites to find Osama bin Laden hiding in caves in Afghanistan, how could Emperor Constantine find all of the "true Gospels" stored in hidden caves and house churches throughout the Roman Empire? It is just not plausible, as *The Da Vinci Code* asserts, that Constantine could "eradicate" every biblical manuscript that taught Jesus was merely a man and replace them with the canonical Gospels.[120]

And by that logic, it's equally implausible that Constantine could eradicate a "quasi-Protestant" primitive Church spread throughout the Roman Empire and replace it with a pagan variant dedicated to things like "sun worship on Sunday." We would expect the "true Church" that practiced a primitive form of Protestantism to constantly be a thorn in the side of the counterfeit "Catholic Church." Yet although there were heretical sects that never seemed to go away, such as the Gnostics, there weren't any that resembled modern Protestantism in their theology or practice.[121]

WHEN CATHOLICS ARGUE LIKE ATHEISTS

We've seen that some Protestants and atheists dabble in conspiracy theories claiming that modern Catholicism and modern Christianity derive, not from Jesus and the apostles, but from the imperial decree of a conniving Roman emperor. And though Catholics may not place Constantine at the center of their own theories, they aren't immune to the allure of implausible conspiratorial thinking.

For example, some Catholics who question or reject much of the Church's teachings given after the Second Vatican Council claim that modern Catholicism is not the authentic development of the deposit of faith given to the apostles 2,000 years ago. Instead, it is the byproduct of a conspiracy to replace the "true Church" with a counterfeit Church. Just as the Roman emperor Constantine tried to replace Gnosticism with Christian Orthodoxy or proto-Protestantism with Catholicism (depending on whom you ask), another Roman leader tried to replace the true Church with a false one: the pope (or at least every pope who reigned after Pope Pius XXII's death in 1958).

The debate over how well Vatican II preserved the continuity of Catholic teaching is vast and far beyond the scope of this book. But there is space to highlight some of the more lurid charges of conspiracy that are as implausible as the charges found in atheistic and Protestant historical revisionism. These include claims that:

- Archbishop Annibale Bugnini was a Freemason who collaborated with other infiltrators during the Second Vatican Council to revise the liturgy in an attempt to destroy it.[122]
- Sr. Lucia dos Santos, one of the visionary children of Fatima, was replaced with a lookalike impostor in order to prevent her from revealing the "true secret" of Fatima.[123]
- Pope John Paul I, who only served as pope for thirty-three days, was murdered to prevent the restoration of the Tridentine mass.[124]

One reason that people are often drawn to conspiracy theories is because it is, as journalists Kaleigh Rogers and Jasmine Mithani note, "a deeply human characteristic to perceive order in chaos."[125] It can also be comforting to imagine order in chaotic events that threaten our sense of personal safety.

For example, the fact that nineteen terrorists armed only with box cutters could kill more than 3,000 Americans in a single day might lead many of us to think we aren't safe in our day-to-day lives. But we are safe if this particular attack were actually the result of a conspiracy within the U.S. government to achieve a foreign policy goal. With that explanation in place, the conspiracy theorist doesn't have to accept uncomfortable truths about weaknesses in security systems or the grim facts of our own mortality.

Likewise, if Constantine simply invented Christianity or Catholicism, an atheist or a Protestant doesn't have to confront uncomfortable truths about how the key elements of these belief systems can be traced all the way back to the earliest Christians who received the Faith from the apostles.

Atheists don't have to explain how the followers of a crucified rabbi ended up thinking he was the Lord of the Universe. Protestants don't have to explain how the successors of the apostles adopted Catholic practices and so egregiously failed to hand on the true apostolic faith. Instead, they take comfort in thinking that there was always a "true church" that believed in a purely human Jesus or a primitive form of Protestantism—a belief later suppressed through conspiracy but surviving in a remnant (that they identify with).

And something similar happens among Catholics who reject the Church's current teaching authority. They either have to accept the uncomfortable truth that the Catholic Church maintained its existence through the Second Vatican

Council and its aftermath or they have to face the despairing realization that the Church was overcome by "the gates of hades" (Matt. 16:18) and so it could not be *the* Church that Jesus Christ established.

Not liking either option, instead they say that the true Church has always existed and even though a conspiracy in the 1960's tried to stamp it out, that Church still exists today as a small remnant of true believers (that they identify with). But, along with being as implausible as the Constantine conspiracy theories, this violates what popes have taught even during the period when these Catholics say the Church was fully visible and taught with divine authority.

In 1873, for instance, Pope Pius IX taught on the perpetual nature of the Church and condemned those who "blasphemously declare that it has perished throughout the world and that its visible head and the bishops have erred."[126] In 1896, Pope Leo XIII said the Church "must uniformly remain to the end of time. If it did not, then it would not have been founded as perpetual, and the end set before it would have been limited to some certain place and to some certain period of time; both of which are contrary to the truth." That's why he also said that "those who arbitrarily conjure up and picture to themselves a hidden and invisible Church are in grievous and pernicious error."[127]

Ultimately, Protestants, atheists, and Catholics should avoid tantalizing conspiracy theories that are only attractive because they neatly support one's previous beliefs about the identity of "the true Church." Instead, we should honestly examine the facts of history and follow them to the conclusion that is true rather than a particular conclusion we hope is true.

7

FRETTING OVER FORGERIES

According to some critics, Catholic claims to authority are built on a historical house of cards. Why? Because some of the documents cited as evidence for the Church's authority are *actually forgeries.*

William Webster says that a series of ninth-century documents claiming to be the teachings of first-century popes, known as the *False Decretals* or *Pseudo-Isidore,* "completely revolutionized the primitive government of the Church."[128] Protestant apologist Greg Allison contends that a forged record of Emperor Constantine gifting the Western part of the Roman Empire to the bishop of Rome, known as the "Donation of Constantine," was "one of the foundational elements in the emergence of the papacy."[129] And Dave Hunt has an entire chapter in his book *A Woman Rides the Beast* devoted what he considers to be Catholicism's "Fraud and Fabricated History."

On the one hand, Catholics should take forgery claims seriously and not fudge the truth in order to defend the

Faith. If a critic is right and a document turns out to be a forgery, we should be upfront about that fact when we discuss it. The document could still have useful historical value (for example, by revealing prevailing attitudes in the Church at the time it was forged), but it should not be cited as if it were authentic.

On the other hand, Protestants should not be too quick to make charges of forgery a staple of their anti-Catholic apologetics, since they also have to deal with them.

The early-twentieth-century skeptic Joseph Wheless declared that priests were "ghostly doctors" who "by their quackeries have created the fiction of the disease [of sin], and who purposely keep the patient opiated and on the crutches of faith."[130] His 1930 book *Forgery in Christianity* took aim at forgeries in the Church Fathers, medieval historians, as well as what he called "Scripture forgeries."

In more recent years, leading skeptical scholar Bart Ehrman has published an academic treatment of this issue called *Forgery and Counterforgery: The Use of Literary Deceit in Early Christian Polemics.* Examining things like fake letters attributed to St. Paul (and even Jesus) as well as the issue of who actually wrote the New Testament, Ehrman claims that "only two authors named themselves correctly in the surviving literature of the first Christian century."[131]

When we take a closer look at these "fakes"—either from atheists or from Protestants who argue like them—we see that none of them pose a genuine challenge to Christian or Catholic truth claims.

WHY FORGERIES AREN'T FATAL

Let's start with a well-known forgery claim related to Jesus and the writings of Josephus. Atheist Dan Barker writes, "At first glance, Josephus appears to be the answer to the Christian apologist's dreams. He was a messianic Jew, not a Christian, so he could not be accused of bias." Barker then quotes Josephus's writings about Jesus (known as the *Testimonium Flavianum*), including passages that say, "He was the Christ" and, "He appeared to them spending a third day restored to life." Barker then asserts, "Most scholars, including most fundamentalist scholars, admit that at least some parts of this paragraph cannot be authentic."[132]

Actually, Barker is right. There is almost no possibility that an unconverted Jew like Josephus would have proclaimed Jesus to be the Messiah or that he rose from the dead. We can be reasonably certain that at least *these portions* of Josephus's writings were forged. Most scholars believe that the more modest parts of the *Testimonium*, like the part saying Jesus was a "wise man," are genuine. But mythicists say that the entire paragraph was added by a later Christian copyist. The documentary *Zeitgeist* claims, "This source has been proven to be a forgery for hundreds of years; sadly it is still cited as truth."

And this isn't the only forgery claim related to Jesus' existence. Some Christians say that Jesus' crucifixion was historical because the Roman government preserved a record of it. But aside from a brief reference in Tertullian's writings, no such record has ever been found.[133] A letter purporting to be from Pontius Pilate to Emperor Tiberius discussing the crucifixion of Jesus, called the *Anaphora Pilati*, is a well-known medieval forgery.[134]

Yet even if we granted for the sake of the argument that *every* ancient, non-Christian reference to Jesus' crucifixion was a forgery, that would not disprove Jesus' historical existence. We would still have lots of evidence from Christian sources, such as the New Testament documents and the Church Fathers. And, as we noted in chapter five,

Josephus's mere silence on the matter should not disprove Jesus' existence, since Josephus also doesn't mention the scandal of Paul's conversion and even mythicists believe that Paul existed.[135] And it shouldn't be surprising or suspicious that sources interested in Jesus (Christians) would mention him and sources not interested in him would not.

Whether the charge comes from atheists trying to debunk Jesus or Protestants trying to debunk Catholic doctrine, a historical argument can't be disproven merely by showing that *parts* of the evidence used to support it are inauthentic. They must show that the primary or necessary evidence for the argument's conclusion comes from inauthentic or compromised sources.

Ignaz von Döllinger, a nineteenth-century priest who rejected the dogma of papal infallibility, believed that the False Decretals were composed in France, not Rome. He also believed that the forger's immediate purpose was not to invent new powers for the papacy. It was instead to "protect bishops against their metropolitans and other authorities, so as to secure absolute impunity and the exclusion of all influence of the secular power."[136] The forger was likely relying upon previously established beliefs about the authority of the pope, which are attested to by genuine writings that preceded this ninth-century forgery.

For instance, the fifth-century Church historian Socrates of Constantinople said that "an ecclesiastical canon commands that the churches shall not make any ordinances against the opinion of the bishop of Rome."[137] And Pope Hormisdas (514–523) certainly had a high view of his own apostolic see and its ability to teach without error (or be *infallible*). He said,

> The first condition of salvation is to keep the norm of the true faith and in no way to deviate from the established

> doctrine of the Fathers. For it is impossible that the words of our lord Jesus Christ who said, "Thou are Peter, and upon this rock I will build my Church" [Matt 16:18], should not be verified. And their truth has been proved by the course of history, for in the apostolic see the Catholic religion has always been kept unsullied.

The lesson is simple: the presence of forged evidence does not annul or dilute the value of authentic evidence for any claim. Protestants defenders of Christianity would not allow themselves to be distracted by such smokescreens from skeptics, and neither should Catholics when Protestants employ them.

WILL THE "REAL AUTHOR" PLEASE STAND UP?

Another area where Protestant apologists sometimes claim something similar to forgery is in some of the writings attributed to the Church Fathers, but with questionable authorship. Prominent examples include pseudo-Ignatius, Pseudo-Clement, and the works of "Ambrosiaster," which were attributed to St. Ambrose until it was discovered in the sixteenth century that they had a different, unknown author.

But it's not a good idea for Protestants to get worked up about attributions that don't reflect literal authorship—because you can find these throughout the Bible, too.

Many scholars believe that chapters 40–55 of Isaiah were not composed by Isaiah himself but were added by a later author. This is often called *deutero-Isaiah* though one could also call it "pseudo-Isaiah." In no way does this prove that these parts of Isaiah, including the famous "suffering servant" passage in Isaiah 53, are not inspired. God can inspire multiple people to write Scripture and then arrange history so that those separate works are received over time as a single work attributed to a primary author. God did this with the book of Deuteronomy, too. Even if you believe Moses wrote most of the book (along with the rest of the Pentateuch), someone else must have written its thirty-fourth chapter, since it describes Moses' death and how the location of Moses' grave is unknown "to this day" (34:6)!

In addition, the bar for reading the Church Fathers is arguably lower, since we aren't dealing with the tricky issues of what is the authentic inspired word of God and how it was communicated. The writings of the Fathers simply serve as a witness of the Church's history and traditions. So, even if "Ambrosiaster" (for instance) was not Ambrose himself, he was one of his contemporaries. We can take his work for what it is and nothing more: an expression of Christian thought during the fourth century that offers evidence for the antiquity of the Catholic faith (such as through his connection of 1 Corinthians 3:15 to the doctrine of purgatory).

Catholics can establish the historicity of their doctrines in spite of forged evidence in the same way Protestants establish the biblical nature of their doctrines in spite of forged evidence. Consider the controversy surrounding the *Johannine Comma:* a portion of 1 John 5:7–8 that most scholars say was not in the original manuscript of 1 John. The modern RSV translation renders the passage this way: "And the Spirit is the witness, because the Spirit is the truth. There are three witnesses, the Spirit, the water, and the blood; and these three agree." But the King James Version includes these references to fundamental concepts related to the Trinity:

> For there are three that beare record in heaven, the Father, the Word, and the Holy Ghost: and these three are one. And there are three that beare witnesse in earth,

the Spirit, and the Water, and the Blood, and these three agree in one.

The Catholic Encyclopedia says of this part that "on the basis of manuscript evidence scholars seriously question their authenticity. The Comma is absent in all the ancient Greek manuscripts of the New Testament with the exception of four rather recent manuscripts that date from the thirteenth to the sixteenth centuries."[138] On June 2, 1927, the Holy Office decreed that Catholic biblical scholars were free to conclude that the passage is not authentic.[139]

Yet there are numerous passages in Scripture that teach the existence of one God, the divinity of the Father, Son, and Holy Spirit, and the distinction between these Persons, which is enough to logically derive the Trinity from Scripture even if no verse explicitly teaches this doctrine in the same manner we see in the Johannine Comma. Once again, the presence of invalid evidence does not refute sound conclusions drawn from valid evidence.

A medieval example of this would be St. Thomas Aquinas's *Contra Errores Graecorum*, (*Against the Errors of the Greeks*), which was written to spur unity between Catholics and the Eastern Orthodox. Unfortunately, some of the patristic quotations Thomas uses to support papal authority cannot be located in extant copies of the Fathers. These may have come from a lost source, but it is more likely that the source Thomas used, *The Thesaurus of Greek Fathers*, inadvertently included margin notes from editors in the main text of quotations. Nonetheless, as contemporary Catholic authors have shown, Aquinas's arguments don't rely solely on these quotations. And in many cases, the spurious quotations can be replaced with equally compelling authentic ones, including ones from recently translated works that were not available in Aquinas's time.[140]

But what about Catholic beliefs derived primarily or even *exclusively* from forged documents? Wouldn't the presence of forged essential evidence for a historical argument deal a death blow to its conclusions?

Let's look at one example. The idea that the pope should have exclusive use of certain lands predates the use of forgeries and can be traced to the authentic eighth-century "Donation of Pepin" (which eventually gave rise to the existence of the Papal States in Italy). At around the same time, someone forged the "Donation of Constantine," probably in response to increasing intrusion from secular rulers. It was cited in the eleventh century during the "investiture controversy" in opposition to heads of state who would personally select the bishops of their kingdoms.

In the twelfth century, the document was used to support papal supremacy even over secular rulers. But this notion, though popular among some theologians in the medieval period, was never infallibly defined as a part of the deposit of faith; and indeed, as Catholic understanding of the papacy developed, this aspect of it was not reaffirmed. It was never defined as an essential part of the papacy, for example, at gatherings like the First Vatican Council.

What's our takeaway from this? A forged document can be used to drive support for an idea that becomes popular in the Church for a time, but thanks to the protection of the Holy Spirit, such ideas have never become defined as part of the Catholic faith.

For another example, consider the fifteenth-century "Letter of Lentulus," which purports to be from a Roman official and contains a physical description of Jesus Christ. It influenced Christian art for centuries (even among Protestants) before its spurious nature was discovered.[141] But in spite of its influence, the Church never defined its contents and in fact has never made any official teaching on Jesus' physical appearance. So, despite the popular influence a forgery might have in a particular era of the Church, critiques of the Church's *teaching authority* based on such examples carry no real weight.

FORGERIES "FALSELY CALLED"

Some Protestants can be so overzealous in their crusade to disprove Catholicism that they end up using forgeries themselves. James White, for example, claims that "the first appearance of the idea of the bodily assumption of Mary is found in a source that was condemned as heretical by the then-bishop of Rome, Gelasius I!"[142]

White is referring to the so-called *Gelasian decree* that is attributed to Pope Gelasius, who reigned from 492–496, condemning a work called *The Assumption of Holy Mary*. But that doesn't mean the decree condemned the *doctrine* of the Assumption. The same decree also declares as apocryphal "the book of the nativity of the savior and of Mary or the midwife," yet no one thinks that Pope Gelasius condemned the doctrine of the virgin birth or any of the traditions associated with the nativity. All we can conclude is that these particular *works* were condemned; not the doctrines that appear in them.

So, even if the decree were authentic, it wouldn't show that this pope rejected belief in Mary's assumption. But it's likely not authentic. According to historian Norman Davies, "Modern scholarship . . . doubts that the decree had any connection with Gelasius."[143]

Along with treating forgeries as authentic in order to find evidence against Catholicism, some critics call authentic works forgeries in order to get rid of evidence *for* Catholicism. This can be seen in Protestants who claim that the early Church was "decentralized" and that believers were organized through "house churches" similar to modern-day home Bible studies. This is flatly contradicted by sources like Ignatius of Antioch (who died early in the second century), who describe Christians being organized under a single bishop who presided over their community. He added that true churches must have deacons, priests, and bishops, and tells Christians that "without the bishop you should do nothing."[144]

Some Protestants are so convinced that this "hierarchical" view of the Church only arose after a later "pagan infiltration" that they insist Ignatius's testimony had to be a forgery from that later time period. The nineteenth-century Protestant critic Philip Schaff said, "The whole story of Ignatius is more legendary than real, and his writings are subject to grave suspicion of fraudulent interpolation." One modern Protestant website says of Ignatius's writings, without substantiation, that "they are all [forgeries written] no earlier than 220 A.D., more likely 250 A.D."[145]

But no serious scholar of Church history holds this view. It is true that eight of the fifteen letters attributed to Ignatius are now known to be forgeries. But in the mid-seventeenth century, manuscripts containing six or seven of the other letters were proved to be authentic. In fact, as the late Lutheran-turned-Orthodox scholar Jaroslav Pelikan said, "It was Protestant historical scholarship that vindicated the authenticity of the seven epistles."[146]

For those Protestants scholars, one of the arguments in favor of these writings was that they did not contain explicit references to Catholic doctrine (e.g. ecclesial terms like *see*), which would be more common in a forgery designed to prove the Church's ancient roots. Note, though, how this resembles the double standard related to the arguments from silence we dealt with in chapter five: if an ancient patristic source doesn't explicitly mention Catholic doctrine, that means the doctrine wasn't believed at the time. But if it *does* explicitly mention Catholic doctrine, then it must have been a forgery, because it contains a later "anachronistic" definition of doctrine! All the same, we appreciate Protestant scholars' verification of these letters from St. Ignatius.

WHEN CATHOLICS ARGUE LIKE ATHEISTS

Catholics should also avoid the temptation to ignore Protestant arguments that include evidence from forged documents. One famous example is the alleged "Strossmayer speech" from the First Vatican Council, a favorite of anti-Catholic Fundamentalist tracts and websites, that argues stridently against the papacy.

In 1870, the Church gathered for the first ecumenical council of the Vatican to discuss, among other things, how to formulate the authority of papal teachings. Sixteen years earlier Pope Pius IX used language commonly associated with infallible teachings to solemnly define the dogma of the Immaculate Conception. Now, the Council was preparing to formally define when the pope could speak in such an authoritative way, but not every bishop agreed with this decision. One of the most outspoken was the Bosnian bishop Joseph Georg Strossmayer. *The Catholic Encyclopedia* says of him:

> At the Vatican Council he was one of the most notable opponents of papal infallibility, and distinguished himself as a speaker. The pope praised Strossmayer's "remarkably good Latin." A speech in which he defended Protestantism made a great sensation. Afterwards another speech, delivered apparently on 2 June, 1870, was imputed to

> him. It is full of heresies and denies not only infallibility but also the primacy of the pope.[147]

Despite Strossmayer's actual speech, the Council went on to vote in favor of the document defining papal infallibility by a vote of 533 to 2 with 56 bishops abstaining. And even though Strossmayer did not agree with defining papal infallibility at the council, he upheld the office of the papacy, as can be seen in an a letter he wrote on the feast of St. Peter in 1869 where he says: "What should I say about the Pope, the visible head of the Church, whom everyone respects not only on account of the supreme power which he holds as the representative of Christ but also for his exceptional qualities?[148]

Strossmayer even was graciously received at the Vatican after the Council as he sought to publicly deny the legitimacy of the forged speech attributed to him that included Protestant Fundamentalist gems like "I have sought for a pope in the first four centuries, and I have not found him," or, "Now having read the whole New Testament, I declare before God, with my hand raised to that great crucifix, that I have found no trace of the papacy as it exists at this moment."

The speech continues to be cited in anti-Catholic literature, including Loraine Boettner's *Roman Catholicism* (1962), Robert Zins's subtly titled *Romanism: The Relentless Roman Catholic Assault on the Gospel of Jesus Christ!* (1994), and countless Fundamentalist websites. You can find it alongside other Fundamentalist fabrications like the story of Alberto Rivera, an alleged former Jesuit priest who claimed the Jesuits were behind world wars and communism before being exposed as a con man by the Protestant magazine *Christianity Today*.[149]

And while it is completely appropriate to point out the spurious nature of the Strossmayer speech and other Fundamentalist fables, Catholics can't merely dismiss the arguments in these works merely because they come from fabrications. For example, it would be tempting to say that the arguments put forward by critics like Zins and Boettner don't deserve to be taken seriously given that these uncritical authors used forged materials in their arguments against the papacy. But by that logic the works of Thomas Aquinas could be rejected because, as we saw earlier, he unknowingly used inauthentic quotes in his arguments for the papacy.

Catholics should simply be prepared to explain not only why these arguments don't come from their alleged sources, but why the arguments also fail to falsify the Catholic faith.

8

DEMYSTIFYING THE MIRACULOUS

In the *Summa Contra Gentiles*, St. Thomas Aquinas says that miracles were more common in biblical times because their testimonial power was needed to establish God's various covenants. They were less common later, but not unheard-of; and Aquinas even cites later miracles as evidence for the truth of Catholicism: "Yet it is also a fact that, even in our own time, God does not cease to work miracles through his saints for the confirmation of the Faith."[150]

This led early Protestants to wonder how the Catholic Church could be in league with the Antichrist if God had performed so many miracles through its saints. The answer for some Protestants was that God *didn't* perform these miracles—they were either pious frauds or demonic deceptions. Calvin called them "frivolous and ridiculous, so vain and false."[151] Other Protestants became skeptical of *any* post-apostolic miracles, even ones that involved fellow Protestants.

Scholar Thomas Kidd describes how a woman named Mercy Wheeler was healed at a Protestant revival service in the 1740s of an infirmity that prevented her from walking. Kidd says that many Protestants could not believe the miracle really happened, because "to eighteenth-century Protestants, miracles were too closely associated with Catholicism, and anti-Catholicism served as an essential component of British Protestant identity. Opponents of the revivals attempted to associate the revivals with Catholic superstition whenever extraordinary claims surfaced."[152]

One recent study of cessationism notes that at the same time, the English clergyman Conyers Middleton "continued Calvin's attack on Roman Catholics by applying Enlightenment historical critical methodology to the miracle accounts of the Church fathers, accounts which had been adduced as support for post-apostolic dogmas."[153] As a result, many modern Protestants adopted the same skeptical attitude that atheists have long harbored against the miraculous foundations of the Christian faith.

COUNTERFEIT CATHOLIC MIRACLES?

Among contemporary Protestants, there is a debate over whether miraculous gifts have continued into the present (*continuationism*) or whether they ceased with the deaths of the apostles (*cessationism*).[154] An example of the latter view is B.B. Warfield's 1918 book *Counterfeit Miracles* that continues to be heralded as one of the standard defenses of cessationism. In his defense of cessationism, Richard Gaffin Jr. says, "The case that I will be making stands squarely in the tradition of Warfield,"[155] and former cessationist Jack Deere calls Warfield "the greatest of the cessationist scholars."[156]

Warfield dismissed Catholic miracles as a byproduct of people who were conditioned to believe the miraculous was commonplace. After all, if everyday bread and wine become the body and blood of Christ through the miracle of transubstantiation, what else could God be doing? "The world-view of the Catholic is one all his own," Warfield writes, "and is very expressly a miraculous one. He reckons with the miraculous in every act; miracle suggests itself to him as a natural explanation of every event; and nothing seems too strange to him to be true."[157]

Warfield explains the healings at Lourdes as the product of "suggestion," and dismissed medieval miracle stories as coming from "the thought of an age so little instructed in the true character of the forces of nature, and especially its deeply seated conception of the essentially magical nature of religion and its modes of working."[158]

If you replaced *Catholic* with *Christian* in that passage, you might mistake Warfield for a "new atheist" like Richard Dawkins!

Warfield's dogmatic denial of miracles becomes even more pronounced when he discusses St. Augustine, who said there were so many stories of relics healing the sick and holy men raising the dead that he apologized to his readers for being unable to record them all.[159] Augustine even describes the healing of a blind man that happened in the city where he lived.[160]

Warfield is suspicious of such accounts because reports of these miracles were not widely disseminated in Augustine's day. He also cites Ambrose and Augustine's testimony that miracles seemed to be rare in their time but had now unexpectedly returned.[161] Of course, if Ambrose and Augustine had that said miracles had always been a common occurrence, Warfield would have probably accused them of having a Catholic gullibility that makes "nothing seem too strange to be true."

But why would we expect these reports to be widely believed?

Scripture records ancient people being skeptical toward miracle claims, such as when the events of Pentecost were written off as the ramblings of drunkards (Acts 2:13) or when people said Christ's miracles were "cleverly devised myths" (2 Pet. 1:16). Even the apostles did not initially believe Mary Magdalene's report that Jesus had risen from the dead (Luke 24:11). Atheist John Remsberg published a book just ten years before Warfield arguing that the story of Jesus was a myth because there weren't widespread reports about Jesus' life, preaching, and miracles among ancient, non-Christian historians (even as denouncements).

Protestant author L. Philip Barnes summarizes Warfield's various arguments that alleged post-apostolic miracles are 1) not well attested, 2) come from secondhand sources, and 3) are supplanted by the advancement of non-miraculous explanations. Barnes then discusses the self-refuting nature of Warfield's approach to miracles:

> The problem, however, is that a number of these negative points would be equally telling if applied to some of the biblical miracles. For example, as Colin Brown has pointed out in his discussion of Warfield's position, the raising of Lazarus, as reported in John 11, is not well attested, being recorded only in John's Gospel, there is no corroborative evidence, other naturalistic explanations could be given, and so on. The point here is not to dispute the veracity of the story, it is rather to note that if the same considerations adduced by Warfield in his dismissal of post-apostolic miracles were applied to some biblical stories, then a similar negative verdict would be required in the latter cases as the former.[162]

In the nineteenth century, Cardinal Newman noticed this selective skepticism among Protestants who rejected

Catholic miracles but had no qualms accepting biblical miracles and even the miracles of modern Protestant preachers:

> It may be taken as a general truth that, where there is an admission of Catholic doctrines, there no prejudice will exist against ecclesiastical miracles; while those who disbelieve in the existence among us of the hidden Power will eagerly avail themselves of every plea for explaining away its open manifestation.[163]

In fact, the desire to "explain away" the data related to miracles can be seen among non-Christians who deny the claim that Christ rose from the dead and among Protestants who deny that the Virgin Mary has appeared to people throughout history.

CHRIST'S RESURRECTION AND MARIAN APPARITIONS

One common atheistic explanation for the Resurrection is that the disciples hallucinated and mistakenly thought they saw the risen Jesus. Protestant apologist Mike Licona argues in response that it would be a "mind-boggling coincidence" for every member of the twelve disciples to have the same predisposition to hallucinations (which makes group hallucinations essentially impossible).[164] Therefore, it's reasonable to believe the testimony of these witnesses to Jesus' resurrection.

But if early testimony from groups of eyewitnesses is enough to show that Jesus was seen alive after his death, why wouldn't the same evidence be enough to show that Mary has been seen alive after the end of her life, in the form of spiritual apparitions? Even atheists raise this point, albeit to discredit Protestant arguments for the Resurrection.

Hector Avalos says that Marian apparitions "form the closest parallel to the Jesus apparition stories . . . Marian apparitions have been reportedly witnessed simultaneously by millions of people, but most evangelical apologists do not see that as proof that Mary is alive."[165] Bart Ehrman provides similar evidence for Marian apparitions and makes this observation:

> It is striking and worth noting that typically believers in one religious tradition often insist on the "evidence" for the miracles that support their views and completely discount the "evidence" for miracles attested in some other religious tradition, even though, at the end of the day, it is the same kind of evidence (for example, eyewitness testimony) and may be of even greater abundance. Protestant apologists interested in "proving" that Jesus was raised from the dead rarely show any interest in applying their finely honed historical talents to the exalted Blessed Virgin Mary.[166]

I once debated an atheist on the resurrection of Jesus, and a member of the audience asked me, "What do you think of the miracle claims of Fatima?" This was a reference to three children who claimed to have seen an apparition of the Virgin Mary in Fatima, Portugal in 1917. After reporting their encounter, a crowd of thousands gathered on October 13, and many witnesses claimed that the sun moved in extraordinary patterns across the sky, changed in color, and that the ground and clothes that had been soaked by rain became completely dry in a matter of minutes.

I answered, "In some respects we have better evidence for the miracles of Fatima than we have for the resurrection of Jesus. After all, the first account of Christ's miracle was written several years later, but the first account of the Fatima miracle was recorded in Portuguese newspapers only a few days later." My opponent acted like this was a damning concession, and it might have been—for someone who denies that Marian apparitions are possible.

Skeptical Protestant apologists who have looked at the evidence for Marian apparitions usually don't dismiss them as hallucinations. Instead, they sometimes-grudgingly recognize that the people involved saw *some* kind of extra-mental, actually existing phenomena.

In a debate on Mary with Fr. Dwight Longenecker, Protestant apologist David Gustafson admitted that "the evidence is quite strong that something supernatural was going on in Fatima."[167] Elliot Miller and Kenneth Samples write in their Protestant study of Mariology that "Any honest effort to provide a satisfying explanation for the phenomenon known as Marian apparitions will prove to be a complex and difficult task. I freely admit that I may not be able to account for everything connected to these unusual occurrences."[168] Even atheist Richard Dawkins says, "It is not easy to explain how 70,000 people could share the same hallucination."[169]

Mike Licona specifically addresses the evidence for Marian apparitions that Ehrman includes in his book on Jesus, asserting that Ehrman has not disproven Christ's resurrection through these examples. That's because, as Licona puts it,

> [Ehrman] merely *assumes* without any argument that visions of Mary are hallucinations. He states that groups had seen her. He admits that many of those experiencing the visions were educated professionals, including doctors, psychologists, psychiatrists, engineers, and lawyers. Even Muslims apparently saw her. And the person perceived as being Mary was even photographed.[170]

In his dissertation on the Resurrection, Licona admits, "For myself, I am not prepared to adjudicate on the matter of Marian apparitions. Because I am Protestant, I carry a theological bias against an appearance of Mary. However, I am not predisposed to reject the reality of apparitions in general."[171]

DEMONIC ENCOUNTERS?

It makes sense that Protestants wouldn't try to explain Marian apparitions with something like an improbable group hallucination, since that would undercut arguments for Christ's resurrection. Perhaps that's why one popular Protestant response to Marian apparitions is that they are *demonic impersonations* of Mary.[172]

Licona says, "Other supernatural forces, such as demons, could be behind some supernatural events in other religions."[173] Miller and Samples opt for this approach, which goes all the way back to sixteenth-century authors like Johann Marbach, who denounced stories of Marian apparitions as encounters with the demonic. "She was a false Mary whom the Jesuits conjured up," he wrote, "with the form and the appearance of the Holy Virgin Mary. [This they performed] through their sorcery and the company that they keep with the devil."[174]

What's interesting about this objection is that seventeenth-century deistic philosophers such as Baruch Spinoza liked to claim that miracles could never be used to prove that God exists because a lesser being, like a demon, could also be the source of the miracle. William Lane Craig says that Christian apologists of this period met this challenge, and that their answer to this question

> constitutes one of their most enduring and important contributions to the discussion of miracles. What they

> held is that the doctrinal context of the event provides the clue to the interpretation of the miracle. It will be the doctrinal context of the event that would be the tip-off whether the source of the miracle is divine or demonic. In so saying they drew our attention to the religio-historical context in which an alleged miracle occurs. And this is absolutely vital. An event without a context is inherently ambiguous. Without a context we have no way of knowing whether the event is just a freak of nature or is an act of God or is the result of some demonic influence.[175]

In my debate on the Resurrection with Matt Dillahunty, I said we should operate with this assumption: *reality is as it appears unless evidence suggests otherwise*. Dillahunty refused to accept this principle, but this refusal leads to all kinds of radical skepticism. If you do accept it, though, clearly at least it *appears* that Jesus rose from the dead. And if that's true, then we are justified in believing that conclusion unless evidence suggests otherwise.

Even during his earthly ministry, Jesus' critics rejected this principle by denying he was a wonder-working prophet of the true God. They said that Jesus "drove out demons by the prince of demons." In response, Jesus said, "Every kingdom divided against itself is laid waste, and house falls upon house. And if Satan also is divided against himself, how will his kingdom stand?" (Luke 11:17–18).

In other words, claiming that Jesus was diabolical *violated basic principles of reason*. Why would an agent of the devil use miracles to motivate people to adopt a belief system ordered toward rejecting the devil? Jesus' healing of the sick and his firm commitment to serving the God of Israel meant that it at least *appeared* he was a prophet. In the absence of any evidence for Jesus' demonic nature, such an explanation (on par with modern claims that Jesus was a technologically advanced alien) is a weak way of *explaining away* the historical data instead of providing a genuine explanation for it.

If this explanation works for Jesus, then it works Catholic miracles, especially Marian apparitions. When it comes to approved Marian apparitions like Fatima, we can ask why the devil would impersonate Mary to move people to believe in a Church whose members promise in their baptismal vows to "renounce Satan, and all his empty works."[176]

Granted, this reply won't be persuasive to a Protestant who believes that Catholicism is truly demonic. When John Calvin was presented with authentic evidence of Catholic miracles performed by a well-respected saint, he merely retorted that it is "one of Satan's wiles to transform himself 'into an angel of light' (2 Cor. 11:14)."[177] Some mighty works may be the result of powerful preternatural forces, but we shouldn't rush to a demonic explanation unless evidence suggests that is the case. In the absence of positive evidence that Catholicism is false, positive evidence like Marian apparitions provide more weight to Catholicism than to other Protestant denominations.

Protestants who believe that miracles did continue after the apostles, and who are open-minded about the evidence for Catholic miracles, must reckon with how it at least *appears* that God is confirming in them that Catholic practices such as the Mass or veneration of relics are true. Catholic philosophers Tyler McNabb and Joseph Blado make this point in the context of events like Fatima:

> We should expect that if a figure who represents a specific Christian tradition appears, then it would give credence to the truth of that tradition (assuming the figure does not denounce said tradition). For instance, if Martin Luther

> appeared with a message from God, then many would consider this to be evidence that the Protestant tradition is correct over the Roman Catholic tradition. Or if John Calvin showed up with a message from God, then this would serve as evidence that the Reformed Protestant tradition is correct over other Protestant traditions (and Roman Catholicism as well). Likewise, the fact that God chose Mary to reveal his message in a Roman Catholic context, that is, a context where heavy Marian devotion is both common and seen as biblical, gives us evidence that the Roman Catholic tradition is correct.[178]

WHEN CATHOLICS ARGUE LIKE ATHEISTS

If Protestants can be dismissive toward Catholic miracle claims, Catholics can do something similar when they ask, "If Protestantism is true, where are the miracles of Protestant saints?"

The demand for specific miracles in order to justify belief mirrors atheists who say that if Christianity were true, why aren't their more miracles among Christians? In response, Christian apologists note that we are in no position to say when God would or would not perform a miracle. The fact that some miracles did happen, like the Resurrection, proves Christianity is true no matter how many other miracles did not happen.

Still, Christianity at least has the Resurrection to vouch for it; what miracles did Luther or Calvin perform? The Reformer's response to this objection parallels Aquinas's explanation for why there was an absence of miracles after the apostolic age. Specifically, that the miraculous was primarily needed during the promulgation of divine revelation and became less necessary when revelation was just being transmitted from one generation to the next.

Calvin said that because the Reformers were not giving any new revelation and were merely proclaiming the same Gospel given by Christ and the apostles, no new miracles should be expected. Or as he put it, "In demanding miracles from us, they act dishonestly; for we have not coined some new gospel, but retain the very one the truth of which is confirmed by all the miracles which Christ and the apostles ever wrought."[179]

The other problem with this charge from Catholics is that some Protestants *do* claim to have performed miracles. Craig Keener's two-volume work *Miracles* describes Protestant missionaries and pastors who were reported to have performed miracles such as healing people and even raising the dead. Some early Protestants even claimed that images of Martin Luther were "incombustible"—they would not burn even when thrown into fires being stoked with Luther's books.[180]

Surely, some of these stories and accounts are false, but that's also the case with Catholic miracle accounts, especially ones written centuries after the events allegedly happened. But to say that no Protestant miracle claim is authentic because Protestantism is false would be to engage in the same kind of prejudice that Protestants like Warfield practice when he says no Catholic miracle claim could be authentic.

But if Catholic miracles prove Catholicism is true, then do Protestant miracles prove Protestantism is true? No, because God may be the power behind a miracle, but his divine act does not necessarily constitute a full endorsement of the miracle-worker's theology.

For example, the apostle John told Jesus, "Master, we saw a man casting out demons in your name, and we forbade him, because he does not follow with us." In response, Jesus said, "Do not forbid him; for he that is not against you is for you"

(Luke 9:49). In other words, the exorcists who did not follow Jesus were ignorant of his true identity, but that did not prevent God from giving them the spiritual gift of exorcism.

As a result, God might perform many miraculous deeds in order to confirm aspects of Protestant theology that all Christians affirm, such as the need to repent and believe in the Gospel. However, when God chooses to perform miracles related to specific aspects of Catholic theology, like eucharistic hosts turning into flesh or when Mary appears to a fourteen-year-old girl and says "I am the Immaculate Conception" it's hard to avoid the conclusion that God is choosing to use signs and wonders to show people that the fullness of the Faith is found in the Catholic Church.

9

APPEALS TO ATROCITY

Some Protestants believe that the Catholic Church is not just spiritually dangerous—it's also a threat to the liberty (and even the lives!) of those who challenge its authority. Fringe Fundamentalists like Jack Chick have peddled all kinds of lurid conspiracies, one of my favorites being that "the name of every Protestant church member in the world" is kept in a "big computer" in the Vatican for future persecutions.[181] And even though most Protestants won't go that far down the rabbit hole, many are quick to share claims of historical atrocities committed by Catholics.

Jimmy Swaggart, for instance, said that "the Roman Catholic church murdered some 20 million people during the existence of the Inquisition."[182] Some online articles push the number even higher, claiming that fifty to sixty-eight million people were killed during the Inquisition. These numbers probably come from sources like W.E.H. Lecky, who said, in typical over-the-top nineteenth-century style, "That the Church of

Rome has shed more innocent blood than any other institution that has ever existed among mankind, will be questioned by no Protestant who has a competent knowledge of history."[183]

"Appeals to atrocity" might be good at raising people's blood pressure, but they aren't good at raising the level of discourse between Catholics and Protestants. That's because they suffer from logical and factual flaws—the same flaws we see when we examine similar atheistic appeals to atrocity made against Christianity and religion in general.

"CHRISTIAN" OR "CATHOLIC" VIOLENCE?

In online discourse, you often hear people say things like, "Religion is the cause of most wars." Richard Dawkins references "the immense power of religion, and especially the religious upbringing of children, to divide people and foster historic enmities and hereditary vendettas."[184] Other critics say that just *Christianity* has uniquely contributed to historical violence. The late atheist Christopher Hitchens claimed that violence was so essential to Christianity that the Reverend Martin Luther King Jr.'s commitment to non-violence meant he wasn't really a Christian.[185]

Before we look at the flaws in atheistic and Protestant appeals to atrocity, let's address an objection that some Protestants may make to such claims. They might say that atheistic appeals to atrocity are valid, but those appeals shouldn't be leveled against *Christianity*. In his book *The Case for Faith,* Evangelical author Lee Strobel interviews several Protestant scholars, one of whom is Church historian John Woodbridge. At the beginning of the interview, Strobel quotes atheist Ken Schei, who says, "Christianity has (by certain people) been used throughout history as an excuse for some of the most brutal, heartless, and senseless atrocities known to man. The historical examples are not difficult to recall: the Crusades; the Inquisitions; the witch burnings; the Holocaust."[186]

Now, some Protestants might reply to Schei that the *Catholic Church* was responsible for evils like the Inquisition and that some of the heretics it targeted were actually "proto-Protestants" who defied Catholic authority. Woodbridge even tells Strobel in their interview that "the Roman Catholic Church has glossed over some things that have been done in the name of Christ and which are obviously fodder for criticism of Christianity in general."[187] But in his review of Strobel's book, atheist Kyle Gerkin expresses the following misgivings:

> While it is true that the Catholic Church has been responsible for many atrocities in its history, there is something a bit suspicious about the way they are brought into the fray here. There is no explicit accusation, yet this is clearly an evangelical book, and I believe they would like nothing better than to plant the seed that it is the *Catholic* Church that should bear the lion's share of the blame. But is this fair? An indisputable fact of human history is that whenever there has been a group with strength, they have oppressed those weaker than them. A people, no matter how bitterly persecuted, become enthusiastic persecutors as soon as the tables are turned.[188]

Indeed, we don't have to go far into history to find accounts of Protestants killing Catholics. This was fairly common in England after the Reformation in episodes like the execution of eighteen priests at the "massacre of Michelade" or the Carthusian monks who were drawn and quartered because they refused to recognize Henry VIII as the supreme head of the Church. Protestants have also used violence against other Protestants—for example, the sixteenth-century Anabaptists who said most believers did not possess valid baptisms. The Lutheran theologian Philip Melanchthon published a pamphlet about the Anabaptists, signed by Luther, concluding that, in some cases, "the stubborn sectaries must be put to death."[189]

To Woodbridge's credit, he does mention evils committed by Protestants—like Luther's anti-Semitism and Southern Baptist involvement in the slave trade. Such examples are why atheists would say that Protestants can't avoid appeals to atrocity by pinning the blame on Catholics. They have to explain their own shameful historical episodes, and in doing so, they leave themselves open to those same defenses being used against anti-Catholic appeals to atrocity.

LOGICAL AND FACTUAL FLAWS

Let's examine the flaws in appeals to atrocity I referenced earlier. First, there is a *logical flaw* in these kinds of arguments. Even if it were true that Catholicism, Christianity, or religion in general uniquely contributed to violence, that wouldn't prove that those belief systems were false.

Consider the common yet false claim that religion has been the cause of most wars. The comedian George Carlin once quipped that "more people have been killed in the name of God than for any other reason." But *The Encyclopedia of Wars* only classifies about 120 out of over 2,000 armed conflicts (or about 7 percent) as "religious wars."[190] It turns out that most conflicts in human history involve disputes over resources rather than dogma and are fueled by nationalist pride rather than religious zeal.

Let's focus on one of those primary causes of war: disputed claims of ownership regarding resources like land. Fighting to reclaim certain lands assumes the truth of the belief that land can be owned. Now, some people might believe it is never legitimate to have things like borders or sovereign states, but that controversial claim wouldn't be proven just because large groups of people have frequently fought over land rights. In other words, fighting over a thing doesn't make that thing illegitimate.

Similarly, many jealous spouses throughout history have killed adulterers because of their passionate belief that marriage is a sexually exclusive relationship. Such acts of violence, however, don't prove that their belief in monogamy is bad or wrong. Those murderers' belief in monogamy could be exactly right even though their actions done in the name of that belief were wrong.

The same is true for religion. That people have, over history, viewed religious beliefs as something important enough to fight over does not prove those beliefs, or religious beliefs in general, are false or bad.

Then there is the *factual problem* with these claims. Appeals to atrocity often rely on exaggerated body counts and shoddy historical inferences that claim one group or idea was uniquely responsible for violence.

Let's take a look at the claim that Catholics (and/or Christians, depending on whom you ask) killed 50–68 million people during the Inquisition. This claim is laughable, given that 25 million Europeans died during the fourteenth-century bubonic plague (or the *Black Death*), a devasting number that constituted one-third of Europe's population. The Inquisition's activities were well-recorded, and reputable scholars give much lower numbers. Historian Edward Peters says, "The best estimate is that around 3,000 death sentences were carried out in Spain by Inquisitorial verdict between 1550 and 1800, a far smaller number than that in contemporary secular courts."[191] Even thoughtful Protestants like Greg Koukl can recognize when an appeal to atrocity against Catholicism defies common sense:

> Early in *The Da Vinci Code*, Brown claims that over a period of 300 years the Catholic Church burned five million witches at the stake in Europe around the fifteenth century. I was immediately suspicious of this "fact," so I quickly took out my calculator and did the math. Rome would have to burn forty-five women a day, every single day, non-stop for 300 years. That's a lot of firewood. Furthermore, a quick Internet search revealed that the population for Europe at the time was about 50 million. If half were female (25 million) and half of those were adults (12.5 million), then something like 40 percent of the entire adult female population perished at the hand of the Vatican. That's more carnage than the Black Plague of 1347, which killed only one-third. Let's just say this seems highly unlikely.[192]

ONE MAN'S HERETIC, ANOTHER MAN'S HERO

Even if statistics of religious violence have been grossly inflated, the thought of even one person being executed for what George Orwell would call a "thought crime" is revolting to most modern people. This is especially true among Westerners who are steeped in a historical commitment to freedom of speech and religion.

The Reformed blogger Tim Challies describes the Campo de Fiori in Rome, where a statue exists to commemorate the execution of Giordano Bruno, a scientist and friar who believed in life on other planets and denied that Christ was God. It was the latter claim that led to his execution, but Challies adds, "There were many Protestants who were likewise put to death right here. The two forerunners of the Reformation and their French and Italian brothers stand in for many other believers who lost their lives for refusing to recant their faith."[193]

Vilifying Catholicism because of the violence its representatives inflicted upon heretics in the post-Reformation period is no different from the atheistic tactic of vilifying the Jewish/Christian God because the Bible records his followers executing heretics. Moses, for instance, ordered anyone who worshipped the golden calf to be put to death (Exod. 32:27–29). Steve Wells, author of the *Skeptic's Annotated Bible*, says, "When the people complain to Moses, he tells them they aren't complaining about him, but about God, making them apostates and heretics, and therefore deserve severe punishment. Religious leaders have used this tactic ever since."[194]

In their critique of religion, atheists like to bring up episodes of Catholic *and* Protestant intolerance, including the time when John Calvin executed the Spanish theologian Michael Servetus because he denied the Trinity. Singing a different tune from his critique of Catholic executions, Challies is quick to offer context and justifications for this practice when done by Protestants like Calvin:

> Remember that we are not dealing here with modern-day Western nations where there was a clear separation between church and state. Religion was inseparable from politics. Church and state were mingled and both rulers and the common man felt that a common religion was absolutely critical to the maintenance of order. In the sixteenth century heresy was a common charge and heresy of the magnitude expressed by Michael Servetus

> was almost always punishable by death. It may be helpful to draw people's attention to the Old Testament where God not only approved of, but commanded, the destruction of entire nations. Surely this would seem atrocious to modern readers, and surely God would no longer command it today, yet at the time it happened it was common practice. The times change.[195]

Challies insists that the Bible can be the word of God even though it allowed evil practices that would no longer be acceptable today. If that's true, then the Catholic Church can be the custodian of God's revelation even though it allowed practices that are no longer acceptable today. The *Catechism* says this about the use of use of violence in Church history:

> In times past, cruel practices were commonly used by legitimate governments to maintain law and order, often without protest from the pastors of the Church, who themselves adopted in their own tribunals the prescriptions of Roman law concerning torture. Regrettable as these facts are, the Church always taught the duty of clemency and mercy. She forbade clerics to shed blood. In recent times it has become evident that these cruel practices were neither necessary for public order, nor in conformity with the legitimate rights of the human person. On the contrary, these practices led to ones even more degrading. It is necessary to work for their abolition. We must pray for the victims and their tormentors (2298).

WHEN CATHOLICS ARGUE LIKE ATHEISTS

No belief system has a monopoly on unjustifiable violence. This also applies to "lack of belief" systems, like atheistic regimes that executed hundreds of thousands of people solely because they were religious. To cite just one example: in 1922, the Soviet Union murdered twenty-eight Eastern Orthodox bishops and more than 1,200 priests. A friend of Sergius I, the head of the Russian Orthodox Church, grimly recalled, "We [were like] chickens in a shed, from which the cook snatches out her victim in turn."[196]

So, when atheists make appeals to atrocities, Christians fire back with an atrocity appeal against atheism. Here's how Greg Koukl puts it:

> Though it is easy to characterize religion as a bloodthirsty enterprise replete with witch hunts, crusades, and religious jihad, the historical facts show that the greatest evil has always resulted from denial of God, not pursuit of him. In the twentieth century alone, Dennis Prager notes, "more innocent people have been murdered, tortured, and enslaved by secular ideologies—Nazism and communism—than by all religions in history."[197]

Dinesh D'Souza likewise claims that "in the name of creating their version of a religion-free utopia, Adolf Hitler, Joseph Stalin, and Mao Zedong produced the kind of mass slaughter that no Inquisitor could possibly match. Collectively these atheist tyrants murdered more than 100 million people."[198]

But Catholics must be careful not to argue like atheists when they make these appeals to atrocity. Even if all these claims were true, that wouldn't prove atheism is false. Moreover, in some cases these criticisms have nothing to do with atheism because the tyrants or regimes being referenced weren't strictly atheistic.[199]

It is fair to note the difference between wartime deaths, many of which come indirectly through disease and famine, and the systematic, state-sponsored executions that occurred in twentieth-century countries like Cambodia or the Soviet Union. But previous wars of religion weren't immune to what we would today call "war crimes." The Catholic attack on Constantinople in 1204, the "massacre of the Latins" that took place in the same city in 1182, and the St. Bartholomew's Day Massacre of 1572 are all involved thousands (or even tens of thousands) of innocent civilians being directly killed or sold into slavery.

When comparing competing worldviews, we should reject the ghoulish standard of simply asking, "Who killed the most people?" We should also condemn the reduction of a complex worldview to stereotypes that make for easy "gotcha moments" like the amoral atheist, the violent Muslim, the money-grubbing televangelist, and the pedophilic priest. We should instead critically examine the content of the worldviews behind these stereotypes to see if violence is an unfortunate deviation from those beliefs or a natural product of them.

10

MEAGER MORAL FRUITS

Do "bad popes" disprove Catholicism? The Catholic dogma of papal infallibility says that when the pope speaks with the intention to definitively bind the faithful to a matter related to faith or morals (this is called *ex cathedra*, or "from the chair"), the Holy Spirit will prevent him from binding the Church to error. But infallibility is not the same as impeccability—freedom from sin. In a way, it's a testament to the dogma of papal infallibility that though there have been morally repugnant popes, never did they formally teach heresy.

Jerry Walls, however, claims that these popes do disprove Catholic teaching on the papacy, because it's reasonable to expect the Holy Spirit to ensure that every pope meet "minimal standards of moral integrity and sincere piety." Some atheists also make this argument, as can be seen in one writer at *The Secular Web* who says, "Even Catholics don't know very much about the popes. If they did, they might well wonder how such an assortment of buffoons and villains could ever have been given the job. Why, it could make one lose faith in the infallible guidance of the Holy Spirit!"[200]

What's problematic for Walls's position, however, is that atheists don't stop there. If the meager moral fruits of bad popes disprove Catholicism, then the meager moral fruits of bad Christians disprove Christianity. But to see why the two arguments are similar (both in their structure and how to answer them) we need to explore Walls's argument in more detail.

THREE "MEAGER MORAL FRUITS" ARGUMENTS

Just how bad were the "bad popes" that Walls says are a clear falsification of the papacy? Walls cites examples of medieval popes who had adulterous relationships, fathered illegitimate children, and bribed clerics in order to be appointed to the papacy. He claims that this is not just a case of "a handful of bad actors," although he only cites the behavior of a dozen popes, which does seem like only a handful of the 267 men who have held the office. Our Lord himself had a higher percentage of bad actors among the twelve apostles!

Walls claims that if the papacy were true, then we'd expect "all popes would meet the basic New Testament standard for bishops, or at the very least be persons of sincere faith in Christ, and basic moral integrity." Why? Because, according to Walls, the pope is "the 'chief shepherd' who is uniquely chosen to lead the church, and who represents a providentially guaranteed succession beginning with Peter."

Of course, this is just an assumed premise on Walls's part. The Catholic Church has never taught that popes are divinely protected from wicked behavior or even that there's any minimum moral standard strictly necessary for a man to occupy the papal office. That means Walls has to give independent reasons to think the Holy Spirit would ensure a moral standard of papal behavior—and conjecturing about God's will is notoriously hard for limited human beings. The Bible says that God's ways are higher than our ways (Isa. 55:8–9) and that no one knows the thoughts of God except the spirit of God (1 Cor. 2:11). Also, any reason Walls gave could be co-opted by an atheist claiming the Holy Spirit would prevent all Christians, or indeed all people, and not just the pope, from engaging in wicked behaviors.

Indeed, just as Walls assumes that the Holy Spirit must ensure that the "chief shepherd" of Christ's Church be free from serious moral defects, some atheists say that God would not have allowed moral defects in the biblical heroes he chose to serve his people—and since he didn't, the Bible is discredited. The eighteenth-century philosopher Thomas Paine wrote in *The Age of Reason*, "Whenever we read the obscene stories, the voluptuous debaucheries, the cruel and torturous executions, the unrelenting vindictiveness, with which more than half the Bible is filled, it would be more consistent that we called it the word of a demon, than the word of God."[201]

Although Paine's argument is rhetorically excessive (really, more than *half* the Bible is obscene?), we certainly can find scriptural examples of God's chosen men acting in ways that make the bad popes look like altar boys.

Another variant of Walls's argument can be heard coming from atheists who apply this reasoning to Christians as a whole. Paul Draper, for instance, doesn't think that God must ensure that *all* Christians achieve the same moral standards Walls has for the popes. There could be bad Christians here or there and this would not count against God's existence. But Draper does believe that, if Christianity were true, then Christians would, on average, be more moral than non-Christians. Atheist Jeffrey Jay Lowder summarizes Draper's argument:

> On the assumption that theism is true, one has reason to believe that theistic belief has significant moral fruits, that worshipping God is a source of moral strength. Thus, on the assumption of theism, the fact that theists do not seem to live more moral lives than atheists is surprising. On the assumption that atheism is true, however, this is not surprising. On atheism, believing in God would not make people morally better.[202]

These two versions of the atheistic *meager moral fruits* argument, as well as Walls's moral argument against the papacy, all share the same basic structure:

1. If God gave a group of people special graces (popes, biblical leaders, believers in general), we'd expect them to maintain a minimum standard of morality (be free from serious moral defect, be better on average than non-Christians).
2. These groups do not meet the minimum standard of morality.
3. Therefore, God did not give these groups special graces.

Walls uses the conclusion of this argument to justify the claim that the papacy is a man-made tradition rather than a divinely appointed office in the Church. Atheists use this reasoning to argue that Christian conversions have natural, psychological explanations rather than supernatural ones, since so many Christians seem to lack graces we'd expect God to give them.

But Catholics can reply to Walls's argument with the same reasons Walls would probably use in reply to Draper.

JUDGE . . . NOT?

Walls sees how his argument could be used against the Bible. He cites as a counter-example the wicked kings of Israel or Old Testament leaders like Moses and David who committed serious sins, even murder. In response, Walls says Moses and David *repented* of their sins, showing they were sincere yet flawed people. The bad popes, on the other hand, were "charlatans" in whom there was no evidence of genuine faith.

Walls also notes that Israel's monarchy was a "genetic dynasty" created as a concession to God's people. It is, therefore, unlike the papacy, which God directly instituted and whose office-holders God providentially arranges. Walls says the more apt comparison is with the biblical prophets—all of whom, he says, met at least minimal moral standards.[203]

But an atheist could still deploy Walls's argument against another group of biblical leaders: the judges.

After God's people entered the promised land, Scripture describes several *shophets*, or judges, who were chosen to lead Israel and deliver the people from being enslaved by neighboring tribes. The book of Judges describes several people God "raised up"—chose—to deliver his people from their oppression. And some of these leaders committed acts on par with the "bad popes" or even worse. For example:

- Gideon led God's people into idolatry by creating a golden Ephod they worshipped (Judges 8:22–29);
- Samson visited a prostitute (Judges 16:1–3) and broke Israel's ritual holiness laws (Judges 14:6–9);

- Jephthah vowed to sacrifice a human being in order to win a battle and ended up sacrificing his own daughter (Judges 11);
- finally, though he wasn't a judge of Israel, the Bible calls Lot righteous (2 Pet. 2:7) and he served as a judge at the gates of Sodom. He offered his daughters to a rape-hungry mob (Gen. 19:8) and later gets so drunk he ends up having intercourse with them (Gen. 19:30–38).

Scripture describes God choosing these men to lead Israel and it never describes the men repenting of these sins. Walls could assume that these men repented of their sins, but Scripture doesn't say it. Of course, a Catholic could say the same thing about the bad popes repenting even if it's not recorded in ecclesial histories. If Walls, who holds to *sola scriptura*, heard the argument from "bad judges" from atheists, he might object to its assumption that biblical leaders must always be free from serious sin, since the Bible never teaches this about them. But if that's a licit move, then we may reject Walls's assumption that every pope would have a such an "unblemished" record.

A similar response can be made to the meager moral fruits argument against Christians as a whole. In this case, it is not the presence of a few grave sins that evinces "meager moral fruits," it is the lack of above-average virtue (though there are probably a fair amount of vices as well). Although we could argue that Christians do meet this standard, we are not in a position to prove it objectively. By the same token, anecdotes about bad or mediocre Christians aren't enough to tell us about whether Christians, as a whole, are morally better than non-Christians.

We could also concede this premise but say the argument still fails because there are plausible reasons for why

Christians might be morally on par with or even worse than non-Christians. God could give virtuous dispositions and actual graces to non-Christians; Christian culture could have a morally uplifting effect on non-Christian behavior; or perhaps the devil tempts Christians to sin more often and more strongly than non-Christians so that they will abandon Christ through their evil behavior.

And those are just a few reasons. Ultimately, we are not in a position to know why God allows Christians to sin even on the same level as (or worse than) non-Christians, or why he allows some Christian leaders, like pastors and popes, to become scandalous obstacles to the Christian faith. And this brings us to another parallel between Walls's arguments from papal evil and atheistic arguments from evil and suffering in general.

THE PROBLEM OF (PAPAL) EVIL

After reviewing the sordid affairs of some medieval popes, many people ask, "Why would God choose these disastrous popes? Why would he choose Benedict IX, who actually sold the papacy?!"

To that I would say: God didn't *choose* these men.

In his omniscience, God knew that these men would eventually become the pope. He didn't positively appoint them to the office, though, but rather allowed the papal electors (such as the College of Cardinals) to use their free will; and he providentially arranged the world so that a greater good might come from any evils involved in their papacies.

Just as the Holy Spirit only protects the pope from formally teaching heresy and doesn't guarantee he will always be the best shepherd, the Holy Spirit doesn't guarantee that papal electors will always choose the best candidate. He simply ensures that the man they pick won't teach contrary to revealed Christian truth. As Pope Benedict XVI put it, "Probably the only assurance he offers is that the thing cannot be totally ruined . . . There are too many contrary instances of popes the Holy Spirit obviously would not have picked!"[204]

But not everyone holds this view. In contrast to this view on papal elections, where God arranges the world just so that the worst papal candidate is *not* selected (Walls calls this the "weak providence" view), Thomas Flint, a professor of philosophy at Notre Dame, has used a *Molinist* account of papal selection to explain the existence of bad popes.[205] Flint says that God can use his *middle knowledge*, or his knowledge of what people will freely do in any given circumstance, to make sure that "the *right* person *becomes* pope" (emphasis in the original). He says:

> If God has middle knowledge, then he knows how any candidate for the office would act—would *freely* act—if elected pope. Using this knowledge, God would then direct the cardinals to select as pope one of those men who God knows would freely cooperate with his guidance and thereby safeguard the church from error.[206]

Under this view, the Holy Spirit doesn't merely prevent a future heretic from being elected to the papacy. Instead, the Holy Spirit ensures that a specific candidate, or the "right person," is elected to the papacy.

Walls, however, is skeptical of both these explanations. Against Flint's approach, he asks why, if the Holy Spirit was actively working through the papal electors, God didn't choose a better candidate. Walls concedes that a Molinist could say there simply were no better candidates at the time, to which Walls says, "I must say I find this suggestion wildly implausible. Surely out of all possible candidates there were better choices to be made."[207]

Replace "candidates" with "worlds" and this sounds just like atheists who say there were better worlds God could have made instead of this one. In his book *Why I Became an Atheist*, former Christian apologist John Loftus writes, "But if God is omniscient, as claimed, then he should know how to create a better world, especially since we do have a good idea how God could've created differently."[208]

For those who hold the "weak providence view" of papal selection, Walls says they might offer a defense he calls *skeptical papism*. In philosophical discussions of the problem of evil, *skeptical theism* is the view that finite, fallible human beings are not in a position to say that God has no reason to allow the existence of seemingly inexplicable suffering (e.g., the Holocaust, animals suffering for millions of years). Our minds are simply too limited and too fallible to know what specific goods God is capable of bringing out of particular evils. But if God is all-good and all-powerful, then we have no reason to doubt that he *can* bring about greater goods, even if we don't know how God will accomplish that end.

Walls agrees the "skeptical papist" could say the same thing and claim we don't know *why* God allowed a certain scoundrel to become pope, but that doesn't prove he didn't allow it in order to bring about a greater good or prevent a greater evil. But Walls finds this, too, "highly implausible, even though it may still be possible in the strict sense of the word." He adds, "The numerous bad popes are a vivid demonstration that the pope is not the vicar of Christ, or the supreme pastor of the Church."[209]

A Protestant might summarize Walls's argument this way: "Sure, it's possible that God allowed these awful popes to be elected in order to achieve some greater good, but c'mon! What's more likely? That God actualized this bare possibility or that bad popes are exactly what we'd expect if the papacy were just a human institution?"

What makes this kind of reply baffling is that Walls doesn't explain why "skeptical theism" is a good (or at least adequate) reply to the general problem of evil. When presented with horrifying evils like the Holocaust, why couldn't an atheist make the same argument: "What's more likely? That God can bring greater goods from serial killers and genocide that we don't know about or evils like the Holocaust are exactly what we'd expect if there was no God to maintain goodness in the world?"

If both arguments have the same structure (i.e. it's possible God allowed a highly unlikely evil in order to achieve a greater good we don't know about), then if one of them fails, the other will fail right along with it.

Yes, it's scandalous that God would allow adulterers and gluttons to become pope, but isn't it also scandalous that a good and loving God would allow millions of Jewish men, women, and children to be gassed in concentration camps, along with an uncountable number of other hideous evils? In fact, in his book *Good God: The Theistic Foundations of Morality* (co-authored with David Baggett), Walls engages atheists on the problem of evil and shows why it doesn't disprove the existence of God.

Walls doesn't say that the idea of God having good reasons to allow such evils is "possible but not plausible." Even in the face of horrors like children being tortured to death, Walls contends that evil does not disprove God's existence. He writes, "Assuming that God sees value in creating a world of meaningful freedom and stable order, it is doubtful that he would intervene often to thwart people's evil expressions of freedom or disrupt the natural order unless the overall balance between goods and evils in the world began to tip in the direction toward evils."[210]

So, if we aren't justified in becoming atheists because God has allowed tremendous evils like genocide to exist in an otherwise good world, then we aren't justified in becoming Protestants simply because God has tolerated the existence of a few tremendously bad popes in an otherwise good (or at least morally neutral) papacy.

WHEN CATHOLICS ARGUE LIKE ATHEISTS

Although Protestantism doesn't have an office comparable to the papacy, some Catholics target the Reformers with illegitimate meager moral fruits arguments. One argument goes like this: if God intended the Protestant Reformation, then its principal leader, Martin Luther, would not have published extremely vile anti-Semitic pamphlets.

Now, it is true that Luther had a very harsh attitude toward Jewish people. In his work *On the Jews and Their Lies*, Luther said Jewish people are "full of the devil's feces . . . which they wallow in like swine."[211] But if this rhetoric disproves Luther's case for Protestant theology, then similar rhetoric among the popes and even Church Fathers would disprove Catholic theology. Pope Benedict XIV (1740–1758), recalling the earlier words of Pope Innocent III (1198–1216), warned that allowing Jews to live in Christian cities would lead to them repaying Christians "as the mouse in the wallet, the snake in the lap, and the fire in the bosom usually repay their host."[212] St. John Chrysostom gave a series of homilies titled "Against the Jews" in which he says things like "demons dwell in the synagogue, not only in the place itself but also in the souls of the Jews."[213]

Could it be argued that since Luther was one of the "founding fathers" of Protestantism, his meager moral fruits are more damning to it than those of certain popes or even early saints (whose place in Catholicism is relatively smaller) are to the Catholic Church? Well, Abraham was the father of the Jewish people, yet he lied to save his own life (Gen. 12:17, 20:2) and had sex with a concubine (Gen. 16:4). St. Peter was the first pope even though he failed to "[act] consistently with the truth of the gospel" by refusing to eat with Gentile Christians (Gal. 2:14).

More importantly, if it is arbitrary for a Protestant like Jerry Walls to deny that God would providentially arrange for a bad man to lead his Church, then it is just as arbitrary for Catholics to deny that God would providentially arrange for a bad man to reform his Church.

Finally, Catholics might be tempted to argue that the Reformation itself has produced "rotten fruit"—moral, theological, liturgical—and so it is a bad tree (cf. Matt. 7:17–18). But although it may be possible in many cases to make a valid connection between Protestant beliefs and certain bad societal fruits, Catholics should recognize the limits of such connections as arguments against Protestantism itself. For only the most naive Catholic can be unaware of the Church's own share of bad fruits—yet we don't believe that these fruits make the Faith false.

11

EMBRACING LIBERAL ALLIES

Some Protestants distinguish Catholic apologists from Catholic scholars or Catholic theologians. According to them, *apologists* gather any kind of evidence, no matter how flimsy, in order to convince people that Catholicism is true. *Scholars*, on the other hand, aren't interested in polemics or apologetics. They just want to understand a certain field of study, and so their conclusions are more modest than those of Catholic apologists.

So, when Catholic apologists make a biblical case for Mary's perpetual virginity, a Protestant might say in response, "Why should I believe that when the renowned biblical scholar Fr. John Meier says that an unbiased historian 'would most likely come to the conclusion that the brothers and sisters of Jesus were his true physical brothers and sisters'?"[214] Or, when Catholics cite 1 Corinthians 3:15 as evidence for purgatory, a Protestant might point out that study notes in the Catholic New Jerusalem and New

American translations of the Bible say this verse "does not envisage the doctrine of purgatory."

James White triumphantly declares that "Roman Catholic apologists know their own theologians are not their friends. In fact, most of their writings are a gold mine of quotes for our side!"[215]

One problem with this approach is that you can find scholars in *any* religious tradition who hold unorthodox views or who denigrate evidence for that tradition (which they accept only for personal or professional reasons). This includes scholars, for example, who say they're Christian but also claim there's little or no historical evidence for traditional Christian doctrines.

For example, Protestants often cite Fr. Raymond Brown's doubts about the evidence for Mary's virginity after Christ's birth, but then they ignore Brown's similar doubts toward the evidence for Mary's virginity *before* Christ's birth (a doctrine Catholics and Protestants both affirm).[216] Former Christian apologist-turned-atheist John Loftus cites Brown in his book *Why I Became an Atheist* and on his blog he admits that "I didn't read atheist works about the Bible so much as I mainly read scholarly Christian literature. What Christian scholars wrote led me to reject Christianity."[217]

So, if it is bad form to cite liberal Christians as expert witnesses against the evidence for Christianity, then it is equally bad form to cite liberal Catholics as expert witnesses against Catholicism.

HOW "CATHOLIC" ARE THESE SCHOLARS?

Let's look at Fr. Meier, a Catholic priest who is best known for his four-volume work *Jesus: A Marginal Jew*. Meier could be classified as a theologically moderate scholar who affirms basic Christian doctrines while expressing deep hesitations about the amount of evidence for them. For example, Meier is skeptical not only of the evidence for Mary's perpetual virginity, but like Raymond Brown he is skeptical of the evidence for the virgin birth itself.

Meier believes, as a matter of faith, that Jesus was miraculously conceived in the womb of the Virgin Mary. However, he disagrees with more theologically conservative scholars over how much revealed evidence there is for this belief. He also says that the Resurrection cannot be proven historically because it's a matter that "can be affirmed only by faith."[218] Such positions make him popular with skeptics and theologically liberal Christians alike. One progressive Christian blogger who denies the virgin birth writes, "As [New Testament] scholar John Meier, who is Catholic and has no reason to deny the historicity of the virgin birth (indeed, he doesn't) puts it: 'We have no clear evidence that the famous passage of Isa[iah] 7:14 . . . was ever taken to refer to a virginal conception before NT authors used it.'"[219]

Indeed, there's no shortage of liberal, self-professed Christians, such as Marcus Borg or John Dominic Crossan, who critique the evidence for Christianity as fiercely as any apologist for atheism or other religions that reject Christian doctrines like Christ's resurrection.

The Muslim apologist Shabir Ally routinely cites these scholars in his public debates. In a debate with Ally on the reliability of the New Testament, James White objected to this, saying that "Ally has adopted the most radically liberal, skeptical, naturalistic sources as the mainstream in Christian scholarship, while using the most conservative forms of scholarship in defense of the Quran."[220] White later wrote an open letter to Ally saying that his "reliance upon the Jerome Biblical Commentary, Raymond Brown, and other notorious liberals who have no concept of allowing Scripture to speak for itself, no concept of the very unity and consistency you asserted for the Quran last evening, remains, and will always be, [his] Achilles heel."[221]

This is rich coming from someone like White, who routinely cites Brown and his co-authors in the *Jerome Biblical Commentary* in order to cast doubt on Catholic doctrines related to Mary or purgatory.[222] In one debate on purgatory, White said, "Hence as Roman Catholic [Fr. Richard] McBrien admits: 'There is for all practical purposes no biblical basis for the doctrine of purgatory. This is not to say that there is no basis at all for the doctrine but only that there is no clear biblical basis for it.'"[223]

White doesn't tell the audience is that Fr. McBrien was a notorious dissenter from Church teaching. McBrien even said that the Church's opposition to female priests made being Catholic feel "like belonging to a private club that won't admit blacks or Jews."[224] The U.S. Conference of Catholic Bishops criticized McBrien's book *Catholicism* because it "gives very little weight to the teaching of the Magisterium" and on several moral issues it "regards the 'official Church position' as simply in error."[225]

WITH CATHOLICS LIKE THESE . . .

When it suits him, White reaches even further back in history to find "Catholic scholars" who support his positions, with the tacit implication that they are authoritative or at least mainstream representatives of Catholic scholarship. In *The Roman Catholic Controversy*, White discusses whether the early Church Fathers believed that Peter was the "Rock" upon which Jesus would build his Church (Matt 16:18). White then refers to how "the French Roman Catholic

Launoy surveyed the patristic evidence" and found seventeen citations of Peter being the Rock, sixteen citations of the Rock being Christ, eight saying all the apostles are the rock, and forty-four citations saying Peter's confession of faith was the rock. White concludes that "if we add these numbers together, we find that the Roman position . . . represents twenty percent of the Fathers."[226]

The discerning reader of White's book would probably ask, "Who is Launoy?" The answer is that Jean de Launoy was a seventeenth-century heretic who endorsed Jansenism (a kind of "Catholic Calvinism") and Gallicanism, which denied the pope's supreme authority and infallibility. He was also apparently not a very careful scholar, either. The nineteenth-century Catholic apologist Fr. Luke Rivington had this to say about him:

> Launoy was a writer of most equivocal reputation. Almost all his books were placed on the Index [of Forbidden Books]. He was committed to various errors on predestination and grace, besides his opposition to the papacy . . . What authority, therefore, can a man like Launoy be on such a question as this? He is certainly wrong in this particular instance; for not seventeen of the Fathers, as Launoy says, but upwards of thirty in the first five centuries, tell us that the rock or foundation on which Christ built his Church was Peter."[227]

Even you didn't know who Launoy was, you should be skeptical of this argument. It naively treats the Fathers as if they each only held one position on the meaning of *the rock* in Matthew 16 and could be divided up accordingly. Yet even modern Catholics recognize that biblical meaning can have multiple layers, and so *the rock* can refer to Peter *and* to

Peter's confession of faith. As the *Catechism* puts it, "Because of the faith he confessed, Peter will remain the unshakable rock of the Church" (552). A. Edward Siecienski, an Orthodox scholar, notes that "four approaches to interpreting Matthew 16 coexisted for centuries, and many Fathers (e.g., Origen, Hilary, Jerome, Gregory of Nyssa, Augustine) happily employed more than one throughout their careers."[228]

Recognizing the foundation of Peter's confession within Christ's true identity doesn't detract from Peter also being the foundation for the Church, since God chose Peter to make this confession. Indeed, the Fathers who identified the Christ as the rock didn't deny that Peter was the rock. For example, St. Gregory of Nyssa said, "The great Peter did not reach such a grace by advancing little by little, but at once he listened to his brother, believed in the Lamb, was completed by faith, and having cleaved to the Rock, became Peter [Rock]."[229]

SCHOLARS FOR ME, APOLOGISTS FOR THEE

For another angle from which to view the double standard at play here, let's look at how Protestants defend their ultimate authority: *sola scriptura.*

In order for Scripture to be a Christian's ultimate authority, he needs to know what books constitute "Scripture." Some Protestant apologists claim that the canon of Scripture (that is, what books belong in the Bible) is not a piece of information we know primarily through tradition, affirmed by an authoritative Church. Instead, the canon is an artifact of revelation, revealed *through the books of the Bible themselves.* The canon thus becomes "self-authenticating," not dependent on any ecclesiastical authority.[230]

To back up this claim, White and other apologists often cite Michael Kruger and his books *Canon Revisited* and *The*

Question of Canon. In the latter book, Kruger admits that his "intrinsic model" of the canon's authority is a minority view among New Testament scholars. He acknowledges that the alternative view—"the canon was an ecclesiastical product that was designed to meet ecclesiastical needs"—is "a central framework that dominates much of modern canonical (and biblical) studies."[231]

But whereas White and other apologists rely on Kruger's work even though it goes against the grain of modern scholarship (since it supports their particular theology), they deride conservative Catholics as mere "apologists," out of step with mainstream scholarship, who advocate for things like a single bishop of Rome in the first century.

Jerry Walls, for instance, claims that "there has been a consensus . . . among historians, including Roman Catholic historians," that there was no papacy in the first century. To buttress his argument, Walls cites Catholic scholars like Eamon Duffy and then charges that "[Catholic] apologists are either unaware of the state of scholarship in their own church, or they blithely ignore it, and assure their readers that traditional papal claims are the uncontroverted truth."[232] In an online interview he doubled down on his scholars-vs-apologists argument:

> I'm citing the Roman Catholic historians. Now that's pretty telling. And again, so far as I'm aware, this represents the consensus among Catholic historians: that Peter was not the first bishop of Rome, there was not a continuous succession of bishops following Peter, as Vatican I would have it. That is not the case.[233]

Walls sings a very different tune, however, when he defends minority scholars who agree with him (like Kruger). In his book *Roman but not Catholic* (co-authored with Kenneth Collins), he dismisses mainstream views of the gradual development of the canon as following "naturalistic presuppositions" that "leave no room for the Holy Spirit's role with respect to the inspiration of these writings."[234] Yet Walls, sees no need to give "room" for the Holy Spirit to guide the development of the episcopal and papal offices in the early Church.

Moreover, citing a few Catholic scholars and claiming a "consensus" is problematic.

First, because it treats other Catholic scholars who *have* argued for a historically continuous papacy as irrelevant to the consensus. Second, the scholars that *are* cited are themselves not wholly relevant to the discussion. Eamon Duffy is a medieval historian, for instance, not a patristics scholar (and most of his argument relies on the work of Raymond Brown). Third, these scholars are often dismissive of evidence for traditional Christian doctrines and not just Catholic ones. Duffy, for example, believes that not only was the papacy a gradual development in Church history, but so was the Trinity:

> The doctrine of the Trinity was forced upon the Church as it struggled to do justice to what God had done for the world. It was forced to the recognition of the divinity of Christ . . . It was forced, slowly and hesitatingly, to recognize the divinity of the Holy Spirit . . . the emergence of the doctrine of the Trinity was gradual, a painful and prolonged attempt truthfully to spell out the stupendous implications of the revelation of God in Jesus Christ.[235]

If Duffy were talking about the "papacy" in this passage instead, you can bet Protestant scholars would share his views, but I highly doubt they would cite Duffy if they were debating the Trinity with a Muslim. If they want to be consistent,

Protestants can't embrace scholars whose methods cast doubt on Catholic doctrines while conveniently ignoring how their same methods cast doubt on Christian doctrines.

Finally, some "Catholic scholars" trumpeted by Protestants and skeptics are so far removed from Catholic orthodoxy that they are Catholic "in name only." One example would be the dissident theologian Hans Kung. In 1979, the Congregation for the Doctrine of the Faith declared in 1979 that Kung "can no longer be considered a Catholic theologian nor function as such in a teaching role."[236] So although his arguments deserve to be taken as seriously as those of any non-Catholic critic, his career of straying from Catholic teaching diminishes his value as a "mainstream Catholic scholar" who can be co-opted in critiques of "Catholic apologists."

All of this shows that just because someone is Catholic or Christian and a scholar doesn't mean he is a qualified or noted authority on the subject in question. In a 2003 debate between Dan Barker and Mike Licona, Barker said that even scholars who believe God exists, like John Dominic Crossan, don't think the historical evidence shows that Jesus rose from the dead. He was trying to imply that Crossan, being a theist, was simply "following the evidence" and wasn't hindered by an atheistic bias against miracles. But Licona pushed back at the idea that Crossan even believed in God, and Barker pushed back with equal intensity.[237] Then Licona referenced a 1995 debate that Crossan had with William Lane Craig, where the following exchange took place[238]:

> **Crossan:** If you were to ask me (which is just what you did) to abstract from faith how God would be if no human beings existed, that's like asking me, "Would I be annoyed if I hadn't been conceived?" I really don't know how to answer that question.

> **Craig:** Sure you do!
>
> **Crossan:** Wait a minute! We only know God as God has revealed God to us; that's all we could ever know in any religion.
>
> **Craig:** During the Jurassic age, when there were no human beings, did God exist?
>
> **Crossan:** Meaningless question.
>
> **Craig:** But surely that's not a meaningless question. It's a factual question. Was there a being who was the Creator and Sustainer of the universe during that period of time when no human beings existed? It seems to me on your view that you'd have to say, "No."
>
> **Crossan:** Well, I would probably prefer to say "No," because what you're doing is trying to put yourself in the position of God and ask, "How is God apart from revelation? How is God apart from faith?" I don't know if you can do that. You can do it, I suppose, but I don't know if it really has any point.

What we see in this exchange is that Crossan may *say* he believes that God exists, but for him, "God" is a kind of interpretive construct formed by the beliefs of human beings. God isn't a necessary being who exists independently of human opinion (or at least Crossan will not affirm that he is). It's no wonder, then, that Crossan doubts whether God raised Jesus from the dead, since people's *ideas about God* certainly don't have the power to do anything!

Kung and Crossan's examples demonstrate that citing a scholar against his own theological tradition has very little argumentative value when his habit of dissenting from that tradition shows him to be a poor representative of it.

WHEN CATHOLICS ARGUE LIKE ATHEISTS

When critiquing another belief system, it can be very effective to cite experts in that system who agree with your points. You just have to make sure the expert you cite is someone your opponents respect, or at least one they don't easily dismiss.

I often cite Protestant sources in defense of my arguments, but I try to do so in a way that doesn't commit the error of relying on "liberal allies" who are barely Protestant in their own right. For example, in my book *The Case for Catholicism* I cited Reformers like Martin Luther on the subject of baptism and modern conservative Protestants like Jerry Walls in defense of concepts like "mere purgatory." I also referenced Richard Bauckham's case that "the brethren of the Lord" (Matt. 13:55–56) were born from Joseph's first wife, rather than Mary because, although Bauckham rejects the perpetual virginity of Mary, he does not see references to Jesus' "brethren" as proof against that doctrine.

But there are many other Protestant theologians whose work is generally considered heterodox by Protestant apologists, and Catholics should steer clear of citing them in "gotcha" arguments. Consider this passage from Protestant scholar Peter Enns who once taught at Westminster Theological Seminary:

> When people read the Bible for themselves, they often disagree about what it means. The Bible does not have a good track record of promoting unity among those who read it. Take us back to the carefree days of the papacy

> and the few who interpreted the Bible for the many. At least you had some order. Now you have chaos.[239]

If you didn't know better, you'd think a) Enns was a Catholic apologist and b) his former position at Westminster would surely vouch for his theological credentials. The problem is that most conservative Protestants, especially those who engage in criticism of Catholicism, would reject Enns as someone with a low view of Scripture who doesn't really believe in essential Protestant doctrines like *sola scriptura* or biblical inerrancy. Conservative Protestant scholar Matthew Barrett critiques Enns in an article whose title adequately summarizes its content: "*Sola Scriptura* in the Strange Land of Evangelicalism: The Peculiar but Necessary Responsibility of Defending *Sola Scriptura* Against Our Own Kind."[240]

Catholics shouldn't stand for Protestants (or atheists) using bad or dissenting Catholic scholars being used to buttress their arguments. And likewise, we should only use the best scholarship from authentic representatives of positions we're arguing against.

12

CRITIQUING CONSERVATIVE FOES

Sometimes Protestants cite liberal Catholic scholars in order to undermine the evidence for Catholic doctrines; at other times, they cite extremely conservative or traditional Catholics in order to make a Catholic doctrine look absurd.

Protestant authors John Ankerberg and John Weldon cite St. Robert Bellarmine's notion that the pain of purgatory is "greater than all the pains of earth put together" even though the Church has no official teaching on purgatory's nature.[241] In other cases, Protestants cite respected theologians and even Doctors of the Church who seem to contradict Scripture. One example would be St. Alphonsus Liguori, who said,

> If God is angry with a sinner, and Mary takes him under her protection, she withholds the avenging arm of her Son, and saves him . . . to Jesus, as a judge, it belongs also to punish; but mercy alone belongs to the Blessed Virgin

> as a patroness. Meaning, that we more easily find salvation by having recourse to the mother than by going to the Son.[242]

The idea that our salvation is found more easily in Mary than in Jesus would seem to many Christians (Catholic and Protestant) to be blasphemous. But it's possible to make any writing look absurd if you take it out of context.

For example, atheists often wrench difficult biblical passages out of context for maximum shock value. In 2012, a Pennsylvania atheist group put up a billboard with an image of an African-American slave next to a quotation of Colossians 3:22, which says, "Slaves, obey your masters."[243]

Other atheists cite traditional Christian authors in order to expose what Christians "really believe" when it comes to their most controversial doctrines. Keith Parsons calls hell "Christianity's most damnable doctrine" and cites the eighteenth-century Puritan Jonathan Edwards, who declared, "The God that holds you over the pit of hell, much as one holds a spider or some loathsome insect over the fire, abhors you, and is dreadfully provoked. His wrath towards you burns like fire; he looks upon you as worthy of nothing else but to be cast into the fire."[244]

Parsons says these and other gut-wrenching descriptions of hell "cannot be dismissed as a morbid phantasmagoria dreamed up by the unhinged or the fanatical. The tortures of hell were soberly proposed by the most distinguished theologians."[245]

ILLUSTRATIVE OPINIONS VS. OFFICIAL DOCTRINE

When critiquing doctrine, we must distinguish an author's *opinion about* or *way of describing* a doctrine from the doctrine's essential elements. James White introduces the topic of purgatory through a lengthy description of a sixteenth-century saint's vision of a fellow religious sister being consumed in literal purgatorial fires because she had "little devotion toward the august sacrament of the altar."[246] It's not hard to find other medieval descriptions of purgatory that rival Dante's descriptions of hell in *The Divine Comedy*. One twelfth-century mystical account comes from a knight named Owen who said that he saw "iron hooks" dragging people across fire, people "baked in ovens and fried in frying pans," and "fiery dragons" along with other animals eating people.[247]

God can give private revelation to individuals, including details about the afterlife, but the faithful are not obliged to accept these revelations in the same way they are obliged to accept public revelation like Sacred Scripture or what the Church formally teaches. Plus, not every claim of private revelation is authentic, so we should follow the Church's guidance and be cautious of alleged revelations that lack Church approval. Those who are critiquing purgatory, or just examining whether it's true, should likewise restrict themselves to what the Church has formally taught about it.

The *Catechism* says those who go to purgatory "undergo purification, so as to achieve the holiness necessary to enter the joy of heaven" (1030). It does add that "the tradition of the Church, by reference to certain texts of Scripture, speaks of a cleansing fire," but the Church has never defined that purgatory involves a literal fire rather than a symbol purification, such as when John the Baptist said Christ "will baptize you with the Holy Spirit and with fire" (Matt. 3:11).

Although some respected Catholic authors, even saints and Doctors, may have written or spoken of purgatory involving gruesome physical punishments, the Church has not formally taught this. But this, unfortunately, hasn't stopped some critics from using these descriptions to prejudice people against the doctrine—in the same way that atheists prejudice people against belief in hell by citing gruesome descriptions of it in the works of zealous, "fire and brimstone" preachers.

Consider when William Lane Craig debated atheist Raymond Bradley on whether the existence of hell is compatible with an all-loving God. Bradley began his opening statement by saying Christians like to antiseptically describe hell as mere separation from God. "This a favorite dodge of Christians" he said, before sharing a description of a boy in hell offered by the nineteenth-century author Fr. Joseph Furniss (or Fr. "Furnace" as Bradley grimly jested):

> But listen! There is a sound just like that of a kettle boiling. Is it really a kettle boiling? No. Then what is it? Hear what it is. It is the blood boiling in the scalding veins of that boy. The brain is boiling and bubbling in his head. The marrow is boiling in his bones.

In his rebuttal, Craig asserted that the chief punishment of hell is eternal separation from God, which is a view the Catholic Church also holds (CCC 1035). Craig noted that "the fiery images from the Bible . . . are one image among many others, and these images are generally taken to be metaphors. I don't have to defend such ridiculous things as what "Father Furnace" had to say."[248]

And he was right. Although Protestants in previous centuries have relished describing hell as an infinite furnace of despair, modern Protestants are more likely to describe hell's punishments as having an interior quality and flowing intrinsically from the sinner's rejection of God rather than flowing extrinsically from some external punishment (such as fire, or a pointy-eared devil jabbing you with a pitchfork).[249] Hell might indeed include such torment, but, in that debate, Craig was only obligated to defend foundational elements related to Christian belief in hell—not any past theologian or preacher's personal opinion on its exact nature.

Protestant apologists who trot out only the most extreme descriptions of purgatory in the Catholic tradition, in order to argue that modern Catholics have soft-pedaled the doctrine to make it more palatable, are subject to the same kind of correction. Purgatory might involve painful external punishments, but Church teaching does not say if it does or what they are. And many faithful Catholic thinkers envision a different, interior sort of purification. In his book *Eschatology*, Cardinal Joseph Ratzinger wrote, "Purgatory is not, as Tertullian thought, some kind of supra-worldly concentration camp where one is forced to undergo punishments in a more or less arbitrary fashion. Rather it is the inwardly necessary process of transformation in which a person becomes capable of Christ, capable of God [i.e., capable of full unity with Christ and God] and thus capable of unity with the whole communion of saints."[250]

READ IT IN CONTEXT!

A friend of mine told me about how he once attended a pro-life event and witnessed a heated argument between a pro-life Christian and a pro-choice atheist. At one point, the atheist said, "Think of your own master Jesus; he said, 'Judge not, lest you be judged.'" The pro-life Christian whipped open a Bible he was carrying, turned it to the passage in question (Matt. 7:1), shoved the book a few inches from her face, and shouted, "Read it in context! Read it in context!"

Although this gentleman should have chosen a different way to communicate his message, his message was right. Jesus never said that Christians can't judge whether certain actions, like abortion, are right or wrong. In the Sermon on the Mount, Jesus was exhorting us to not be hypocrites who condemn people for sins we ourselves commit. I understand this man's frustration, because it can be infuriating to see something you admire be twisted to say something it doesn't say. This often happens with Catholic authors, but let's look at how atheists often use the same technique against Christianity itself.

It happens when atheists claim that Jesus encouraged mutilation by saying, "If your right hand causes you to sin, cut it off and throw it away; it is better that you lose one of your members than that your whole body go into hell" (Matt. 5:30). Or that Jesus promoted family hatred when he said, "If anyone comes to me and does not hate his own father and mother and wife and children and brothers and sisters, yes, and even his own life, he cannot be my disciple" (Luke 14:26). (In that latter example, Dan Barker claims he's not taking a verse out of context, because "the Greek word here is *miseo,* which means simply 'hate,' not 'love less than me,' as some suggest."[251])

In these cases, Protestants recognize that Jesus is using hyperbole and figures of speech for rhetorical effect. Norm Geisler, for example, emphatically says that Jesus never "intended [his listeners] to literally cut off their hands and pluck out their eyes if they offended them (vv. 29–30)!"[252] And when it comes to "hating" one's family, Barker is correct that the Greek word *miseo* roughly corresponds to the English word *hate.* But a word's meaning is also determined by its common usage and by context—not just its dictionary definition.

For example, Protestant scholar D.A. Carson admits that the meaning of the word *worship* has changed over time and didn't always refer to absolute devotion to a deity. The 1552

Anglican Book of Common Prayer, for instance, instructs a groom to tell his bride on his wedding day, "With my body I thee worship," which Carson agrees does not make her a goddess! He concludes that "in all such usages one is concerned with the 'worthiness' or the 'worthship' (Old English *weorthscipe*) of the person or thing that is reverenced."[253]

Likewise, Jesus' use of the word *hate* in these verses does not correspond to the narrow, modern sense of the word's meaning of harboring malice toward someone. In Jesus' context, hate meant "to love less," in accord with a common Jewish idiom. Genesis 29:30–31 says the patriarch Jacob "loved Rachel more than Leah, and served Laban for another seven years. When the Lord saw that Leah was hated, he opened her womb; but Rachel was barren."

In the midst of that family drama, it's important to remember that Jacob didn't literally *hate* Leah. He just loved her less than Rachel, who was the woman he originally wanted to marry before his uncle tricked him into marrying Leah. That's why Matthew uses different phrasing to get Jesus' point across in a clearer, albeit less blunt way: "Whoever loves father or mother more than me is not worthy of me, and whoever loves son or daughter more than me is not worthy of me; and whoever does not take up his cross and follow after me is not worthy of me" (Matt 10:37–38).

PRINCIPLE BEFORE PASSION

Now that we see how important context is, let's return to the passage from Alphonsus Liguori. Just as Jesus would not break the Commandments by telling people to dishonor their parents, Liguori would not contradict the Church's teaching that Christ alone merits our salvation on the cross. Liguori says, "We more easily find salvation by having recourse to the mother than by going to the son," but he then makes this qualification (which Protestants usually fail to quote): "not as if Mary was more powerful than her son to save us, for we know that Jesus Christ is our only Savior, and that he alone by his merits has obtained and obtains salvation for us."[254]

St. Louis de Montfort is another author Protestants bring up as an example of Marian excess that borders on idolatry. One Protestant cites the following passage as his smoking gun for Church-approved Mariolatry: "Let me remind you again of the dependence shown by the three divine Persons on our Blessed Lady. Theirs is the example which fully justifies our dependence on her."[255] The Protestant critic then asks, "Do Roman Catholics acknowledge Mary as Lord and Master of everything that exists? Yes they do."[256]

But in the cited passage, de Montfort goes on to explain that he is talking about dependence in regard to her role in the Incarnation, not absolute metaphysical dependence as if the Trinity could not exist without Mary. Far from that, de Montfort clearly articulates Mary's inconsequential status before God:

> With the whole Church I acknowledge that Mary, being a mere creature fashioned by the hands of God is, compared to his infinite majesty, less than an atom, or rather is simply nothing, since he alone can say, "I am he who is." Consequently, this great Lord, who is ever independent and self-sufficient, never had and does not now have any absolute need of the Blessed Virgin for the accomplishment of his will and the manifestation of his glory. To do all things he has only to will them.[257]

People naturally choose their words differently depending on the setting, and we should take the setting into account when we judge those words.

Imagine that my wife is on trial and I have been called as a witness in her defense. I know beyond a doubt she is innocent, but when I'm on the stand I won't say exactly how I feel. That's because I know the prosecutor is ready to take any of my words and use them against me. Even well-meaning praise can get twisted to mean the opposite of what I intended to say, so I'm going to use very measured and precise language when dealing with him. But when I'm speaking to my wife directly, or to our mutual friends, I have no problem speaking passionately and without reservation.

Christian authors, both Catholic and Protestant, often carefully qualify their words when before skeptical and hostile audiences, but speak without reservation when they address a friendly audience or even God himself in a prayer that might later be shared with others. It's not that they're more authentic or truthful in the second setting; they're just less careful about the consequences that imprecision or exaggeration might cause in front of a more hostile audience. As a result, fairness demands we critique a theology based on what it officially teaches—by what it "presents before the court"—and not on the less-guarded statements of some of its devotees.

WHEN CATHOLICS ARGUE LIKE ATHEISTS

We've already seen how some Marian theology can take on rhetorical flourishes when presented outside the context of a Catholic/Protestant debate. But the same thing can be found in Protestant writings and Catholics must be careful to not pounce on those examples as definitive proof of the errors of Protestantism. One of the most famous is this quote from Martin Luther: "Be a sinner and sin boldly. . . . No sin will separate us from the Lamb, even though we commit fornication and murder a thousand times a day."

This can make it sound like Luther believed in such a strong view of justification by faith alone that faith could save a person even if he lived the most depraved life imaginable—even *encouraging* such depravity as a kind of perverse test. But Luther did not believe that our conduct has no effect on our salvation. In fact, he argued against the antinomians who believed that Christians had no duty to keep the Ten Commandments, and he said that salvation could be lost through sins like apostasy.[258]This notorious passage comes from a letter he wrote to his like-minded friend Philip Melanchthon. Here is the fuller context:

> Be a sinner and sin boldly, but believe and rejoice in Christ even more boldly, for he is victorious over sin, death, and the world. As long as we are here [in this world] we have to sin. This life is not the dwelling place of righteousness, but, as Peter says, we look for new heavens and a new earth in which righteousness dwells. It is enough that by the riches of God's glory we have come to know the Lamb that takes away the sin of the world. No sin will separate us from the Lamb, even though we commit fornication and murder a thousand times a day. Do you think that the purchase price that was paid for the redemption of our sins by so great a Lamb is too small?

Protestant scholars recognize that Luther is being hyperbolic when he talks about sin being unable to separate us from God. The context of this letter was to encourage Melanchthon in exercising his leadership role in Wittenberg and to not be afraid of making mistakes. According to Luther biographer Eric Metaxas:

> Luther was hardly saying that Melanchthon should try to sin, as many have misinterpreted quotation, but that he should forget about trying not to sin, because in the end this was not possible. He must understand that in all that we do, we will doubtless sin—because we are sinners—but if your faith is in Christ, who has already defeated sin and paid for our sins on the cross, we are redeemed.[259]

Obviously, this isn't something Luther would say in one of his famous public disputes with Catholic theologians, but it makes sense in the personal context of a letter to a friend.

Finally, both Catholics and Protestants need to be wary of citing theological opinions as if they were a religion's official doctrines. For example, in 1909 the Mormon Church declared that "The Father of Jesus is our Father also. . . . Jesus, however, is the first-born among all the sons of God—the first begotten in the spirit, and the only begotten in the flesh."[260]

Some early Mormons took this to mean that Heavenly Father (whom Mormons believe is an exalted man who has a physical body) had physical intercourse with the Virgin Mary. Brigham Young said that Jesus was "begotten of his Father, as we were of our fathers."[261] However, the modern Mormon church has no teaching on how Jesus was conceived in his mother's womb, so Young's statement should be treated as a theological opinion within Mormonism and not be used as a damning example of Mormon doctrine.

Like all of the examples we've discussed throughout this book, a Catholic would do well to follow the Golden Rule: if you would roll your eyes at a critic treating an unofficial (or downright eccentric) witness of Catholic doctrine as if his views were on par with the *Catechism*, then don't do the same thing toward Protestants, or any religion for that matter. We should judge the truth of a religion on whether its official teachings correspond to reality, not on how shocked we are by the opinions of some of its adherents.

CONCLUSION

CAN PROTESTANTS *WAGER* LIKE ATHEISTS?

During my interview with Cameron Bertuzzi that served as the catalyst for this book, I noticed one similarity between Protestants and atheists that was not a cause for concern (like the twelve similarities we previously looked at) but a cause for *hope*. Cameron asked me what a Protestant should do if he finds Catholicism attractive but still can't overcome certain intellectual hurdles to the Catholic faith.

I asked him in response, "Well, what would you tell an atheist who said the same thing about Christianity? Imagine an atheist told you he thinks the Christian story is beautiful and he desperately wants it to be true, but he just doesn't believe it's true. At least not yet."

Both of us agreed that we would probably encourage an atheist to believe in Christianity (or at least to act like

Christianity were true) and to give it an opportunity to become more intelligible to him. After all, a person who chooses such an approach has nothing to lose and everything to gain.

You may already be familiar with this practical approach to belief in God, called *Pascal's Wager,* and I told Cameron I would offer this same "wager" to a Protestant who wants Catholicism to be true.

"WAGER, THEN, WITHOUT HESITATION"

In his work *Pensées*, the French word for "thoughts," the seventeenth-century mathematician and essayist Blaise Pascal put forward several arguments for the existence of God. However, he didn't consider any of them capable of swaying a truly undecided person. So, what should a person do if he's honestly "on the fence" regarding theism? Pascal offers this advice:

> To which side shall we incline? Reason can decide nothing here. There is an infinite chaos which separated us. A game is being played at the extremity of this infinite distance where heads or tails will turn up. What will you wager? . . . Let us weigh the gain and the loss in wagering that God is. Let us estimate these two chances. If you gain, you gain all; if you lose, you lose nothing. Wager, then, without hesitation that he is.[262]

Many people misunderstand Pascal's Wager as being primarily about avoiding hell. They think Pascal is saying the following:

> Believe in God because, if God exists, you get go to heaven. And if you're wrong about God existing, you'll never know

> you were wrong, because you won't survive your own death. But if you don't believe in God, then even if you are correct you'll never know you were right (because, once again, you won't survive your own death). But whereas no harm comes from being wrong about God existing, there is a harm that can come from being wrong about God not existing. In fact, you'll have a horrifying eternity to contemplate your error, since you'll be in hell forever. Therefore, believing in God is the safest "bet" you can make.

But this formulation of the wager is vulnerable to an objection called the "wrong hell problem." It goes like this:

> If I believe in God simply to avoid ending up in hell, then which God should I worship? What if I go to hell because I worshipped the wrong God, and the true God would've had mercy on me if I hadn't believed in a false one? How do I know which God to believe in, given that human beings have worshipped thousands of them since the dawn of civilization?

However, Pascal would say that this objection doesn't apply to his wager, because he isn't proposing that we believe in God in order to avoid hell. Rather than being a maneuver to avoid harm after death, the wager is meant to avoid *missing out on the good* of the Christian life. You not only get heaven if Christianity turns out to be true; the cost of belief is justified by what you also gain in this life by being a faithful believer. Here's how Pascal puts it:

> Now, what harm will befall you in taking this side? You will be faithful, honest, humble, grateful, generous, a sincere friend, truthful. Certainly you will not have those

> poisonous pleasures, glory and luxury; but will you not have others? I will tell you that you will thereby gain in this life, and that, at each step you take on this road, you will see so great certainty of gain, so much nothingness in what you risk, that you will at last recognize that you have wagered for something certain and infinite, for which you have given nothing.

Pascal would say that, when it comes to believing in God, you have everything to gain and nothing significant to lose. But when it comes to disbelief, there is nothing comparable to gain, so it's not the pragmatic choice. And in fact, a recent Pew study has shown that in the United States, 36 percent of actively religious people say they are "very happy" compared to 25 percent of religiously unaffiliated people.[263]

Pascal's Wager was not meant for the hardened atheist who thinks all religions have basically the same lack of evidence. It was instead meant for a person who has weighed the options and is stuck on a choice between atheism or Christianity, but they would be very happy if Christianity turned out to be true. In that case, if two beliefs seem equally likely, there's nothing wrong with "wagering" on the belief a person wants to be true.

A WAGER FOR PROTESTANTS?

Just as Pascal's Wager will only be persuasive for certain kinds of non-Christians, the Protestant version of the wager will only be persuasive for certain kinds of Protestants—for example, those who want Catholicism to be true because they see it as offering unique spiritual goods they can't have outside the Church (e.g., a robust view of the real presence of Christ in the Eucharist).

Conversely, the wager would have a very minimal effect on a Protestant who believes that Catholicism is not a Christian religion. If he thinks that Catholics risk their eternal souls by following Church teaching, then he definitely has "much to lose" in any bet on Catholicism. This would parallel an atheist who thinks worshipping the Christian God might offend some other deity, and so he'd rather not take the chance and remain in a state of non-belief. But if a Protestant thinks Catholics no more risk going to hell than Methodists or Presbyterians, then the wager could be very persuasive.

But what if someone believes that people in all Christian traditions stand an equal chance of going to heaven? Does the Protestant version of Pascal's Wager lose its force?

In the classic version of the wager, there is a difference of infinite value between choosing Christianity and choosing atheism. Pascal says an atheist should bet on Christianity because of the goods he will receive not only in this life, but also in the life to come. "If you gain, you gain all; if you lose, you lose nothing" he tells us. Pascal would not that say atheism is an equal bet through which one could "gain all." Even if it were possible for an atheist to be saved, this would be in spite of his "bet" on atheism, not because of it.

However, many Christians believe that people can "gain all," or be saved, whether they are Catholic or Protestant (and they may see the spiritual goods in this life as roughly on par, as well). Such people might fairly wonder why the wager would be worth the bother.

But just as it is only *possible* that an atheist can be saved in spite of his ignorance about the necessity of being united to Christ in baptism, it is only *possible* that a Protestant can be saved in spite of his ignorance of the necessity of being united to Christ's Church through the reception of sacraments like the Eucharist. In the Gospel of John, Jesus says, "You will die in your sins unless you believe that I am he [who has come]" (8:24), and "unless you eat the flesh of the Son of man and drink his blood, you have no life in you" (6:53).

God is merciful toward those who fail to obey these commands due to invincible ignorance, but we shouldn't presume upon his mercy. That means an atheist who is on the fence about Christianity, or a Protestant who is on the fence about Catholicism, may have to depart from the classic version of Pascal's Wager and factor the infinite losses he may suffer if he rejects God's will for his life into his decision.

I BELIEVE, HELP MY UNBELIEF!

Finally, some Protestants may face an *obstacle of the will*: they want Catholicism to be true, but they just aren't convinced it is true. Moreover, it seems impossible merely to will yourself to believe something if you don't already think it's true. Believing seems to be something that "just happens," and so it's beyond our control. My advice to Protestants, though, would mirror my advice to atheists who want Christianity to be true but seem unable to believe it is true.

First, don't reduce the faith you want to accept to certain practices of the faith that are not essential to it. Sometimes what outsiders find difficult to accept is not Catholicism or Christianity itself, but a particular *expression* of those beliefs, or ancillary beliefs or practices that seem to go along with it.

For example, I would say that if someone believes Jesus is God but can't accept "young-earth creationist" claims about the earth only being a few thousand years old (popular among some segments of Christians), then he should simply be a Christian who rejects young-earth creationism. The age of the earth isn't an essential Christian doctrine. Christians, including Catholics, are free to affirm beliefs like young-earth creationism, but they aren't obligated to affirm those beliefs.

A Protestant might have a hard time accepting certain aspects of the philosophy of St. Thomas Aquinas. But although the Church holds Aquinas's thought in especially high esteem, a Catholic isn't obligated to be a Thomist. He might, instead, accept alternative but still perfectly valid philosophical approaches from people like St. Bonaventure or Bl. John Duns Scotus if they are easier to accept.

This also applies to a whole host of Catholic devotional practices, even the most widespread ones, like praying the rosary, that can be fruitful but are not mandatory. If a person isn't spiritually attracted to a given devotion, he may try others: such as praying the Liturgy of the Hours, or a scriptural set of prayers called *lectio divina*, or many others—or just offering spontaneous prayers in a prayer corner at home. Pope John XXIII recalled a common saying on these matters: "In essentials, unity; in doubtful matters, liberty; in all things, charity."[264]

In no case should an aversion to any such non-essential practice be a cause for rejecting Catholicism altogether.

This means that a Protestant who is contemplating this wager should learn what is an essential teaching of the Catholic faith that must be believed, such as Christ's real presence in the Eucharist, and what is a practice that people can have differing opinions about, such as which kind of worship or liturgy a person prefers. One way to do that is to read a good summary of what Catholicism teaches, like *The Compendium of the Catechism of the Catholic Church.*

Second, I would encourage a person who is having doubts about particular doctrines or practices to find a *spiritual mentor.* A mentor who is also a convert can be especially helpful because he can guide the person down a path he already traveled and share how he overcame similar obstacles. Pascal offers similar advice:

> Try therefore to convince yourself, not by piling up proofs of God, but by subduing your passions. You desire to attain faith, but do not know the way. You would like to cure yourself of unbelief, and you ask for remedies. Learn of those who were bound and gagged like you, and who now stake all they possess. They are men who know the road you desire to follow, and who have been cured of a sickness of which you desire to be cured. Follow the way by which they set out, acting as if they already believed, taking holy water, having masses said, etc. Even this will naturally cause you to believe and bunt your cleverness.

Finally, Pascal implies that the best way to overcome doubts is to "dive into them." Sometimes we can't truly understand a faith we admire until we "put it on" and live it out, at least for a short period of time. I'm not that saying a person should be a relativist and just believe whatever he wants to be true. I'm saying that if he wants something like Christianity or Catholicism to be true, but his heart isn't fully on board with the idea, then moving forward might require more than just intellectual deliberations.

He may need to just act as if the Faith *were* true, and *will* to be Catholic even if he isn't fully convinced. This would be similar to "willing" to love someone you know you *ought* to love (like an estranged relative) even if you don't have loving *feelings* toward that person. Eventually, if the feelings are natural and ordered, they often "catch up" with the will so that one no longer acts out of duty, but out of genuine love and conviction.

I'll close with advice from C.S. Lewis—written for an atheist but equally applicable to a Protestant who wants Catholicism to be true:

> When you are not feeling particularly friendly but know you ought to be, the best thing you can do, very often, is to put on a friendly manner and behave as if you were a nicer person than you actually are. And in a few minutes, as we have all noticed, you will be really feeling friendlier than you were. Very often the only way to get a quality in reality is to start behaving as if you had it already. . . . Now, the moment you realize, "Here I am, dressing up as Christ," it is extremely likely that you will see at once some way in which at that very moment the pretense could be made less of a pretense and more of a reality.[265]

ABOUT THE AUTHOR

After his conversion to the Catholic faith, Trent Horn earned master's degrees in the fields of theology, philosophy, and bioethics. He serves as a staff apologist for Catholic Answers, where he specializes in teaching Catholics to graciously and persuasively engage those who disagree with them. Trent models that approach each week on the radio program *Catholic Answers Live* and on his own podcast, *The Counsel of Trent*. Trent has written for the *National Catholic Bioethics Quarterly*, and is the author of nine books, including *Answering Atheism* and *Why We're Catholic: Our Reasons for Faith, Hope, and Love*.

ENDNOTES

1 I acknowledge that showing Protestantism to be false does not prove that Catholicism is true. Once someone recognizes that God's revelation is not confined to Scripture alone but also exists in Sacred Tradition, he will have to discern whether that Tradition is found in the Catholic Church or the Eastern Orthodox churches.

2 "John Shook v. William Lane Craig Debate: 'Does God Exist?'" (30:23), available online at: https://www.youtube.com/watch?v=Wf9-vwnzqOo.

3 Sophie Roell, "The Best Books on Atheism Recommended by Susan Jacoby," Five Books, available online at: https://fivebooks.com/best-books/susan-jacoby-on-atheism/.

4 "EPIC Debate on Sola Scriptura w/ Patrick Madrid & James White" (13:32–14:16), available online at: https://www.youtube.com/watch?v=LlLlzDBHhhA. However, Madrid pointed out that they were debating the resolution "Does the Bible teach *sola scriptura*?" As a result, Madrid said, "Mr. White, tonight this Bible is your universe. This is what you have to search. You don't have to go to any other planets tonight, Mr. White. I invite you to stay right here on planet Earth and simply show us where in the Bible the doctrine of *sola scriptura* is found" (38:31).

5 "Greg Koukl: Sola Scriptura," available online at: https://www.youtube.com/watch?v=zyHU-ZCKO-E.

6 Frank Turek, *Stealing from God: Why Atheists Need God to Make Their Case* (Colorado Springs, CO: NavPress, 2014), xxiv.

7 Ibid. xviii.

8 Gregory Koukl, *Tactics: A Game Plan for Discussing Your Christian Convictions* (Grand Rapids: Zondervan, 2009), 174.

9 Paul Copan, "The Presumptuousness of Atheism," available online at: http://www.paulcopan.com/articles/pdf/presumptuousness-of-atheism.pdf.

10 C.S. Lewis, *Mere Christianity* (New York: Harper Collins, 1952), VIII.

11 William Lane Craig, "#592 Is Mere Christianity Sufficient for Salvation?," *Reasonable Faith* (August 19, 2018), available online at: https://www.reasonablefaith.org/question-answer/P20/is-mere-christianity-sufficient-for-salvation.

12 Normal L. Geisler and Frank Turek, *I Don't Have Enough Faith to Be an Atheist* (Wheaton, IL: Crossway Books, 2004), 364.

13 Ibid., 365.

14 Ibid., 368.

15 Lee Martin McDonald, *The Biblical Canon: Its Origin, Transmission, and Authority* (Grand Rapids, MI: Baker Academic, 2007), 418, 383.

16 Michael Kruger, *Canon Revisited: Establishing the Origins and Authority of the New Testament Books* (Wheaton, IL: Crossway, 2012), 46.

17 Letter to the Trallians, 2.

18 1 Clement, 44.

19 *Against Heresies*, 3.3.2–3.

20 Lee Martin McDonald, *The Biblical Canon: Its Origin, Transmission, and Authority* (Grand Rapids, MI: Baker Academic, 2007), 296.

21 Westminster Confession of Faith, 1.6, Center for Reformed Theology and Apologetics, available online at: http://www.reformed.org /documents/wcf_with_proofs/.

22 Gregory Koukl, *Tactics: A Game Plan for Discussing Your Christian Convictions* (Grand Rapids: Zondervan, 2009), 139.

23 "Greg Koukl: *Sola Scriptura*," available online at: https://www.youtube.com/watch?v=zyHU-ZCKO-E.

24 Charles Hodge, *Systematic Theology*, vol. 1.1

25 Normal L. Geisler and Frank Turek, *I Don't Have Enough Faith to Be an Atheist* (Wheaton, IL: Crossway Books, 2004), 127.

26 Norman L. Geisler and Ralph E. MacKenzie, *Roman Catholics and Evangelicals: Agreements and Differences* (Grand Rapids, MI: Baker Books, 1995), 178.

27 Matthew Barrett, *God's Word Alone: The Authority of Scripture* (Grand Rapids, MI: Zondervan, 2016), 334.

28 Ibid., 193.

29 Ibid., 187.

30 *Summa Theologiae*, 1.68.3.

31 Norman L. Geisler and Ralph E. MacKenzie, *Roman Catholics and Evangelicals: Agreements and Differences* (Grand Rapids, MI: Baker Books, 1995), 194.

32 "Imagine playing 'telephone' not in a solitary living room with ten kids on a sunny afternoon in July, but over the expanse of the Roman Empire (some 2,500 miles across!), with thousands of participants, from different backgrounds,

with different concerns, and in different contexts, some of whom have to translate the stories into different languages all over the course of decades. What would happen to the stories?" Bart D. Ehrman, *Jesus: Apocalyptic Prophet of the New Millennium* (New York: Oxford University Press, 1999), 52.

33 Normal L. Geisler and Frank Turek, *I Don't Have Enough Faith to Be an Atheist* (Wheaton, IL: Crossway Books, 2004), 245.

34 Ibid., 246.

35 "The Church has received the tradition from the apostles to give baptism even to little children. For they to whom the secrets of the divine mysteries were committed were aware that in everyone was [original] sin's innate defilement, which needed to be washed away through water and the Spirit." Origen, *Commentary on Romans, 5.9.* This translation can be found in Thomas Scheck, *Origen: Commentary on the Epistle to the Romans Books 1–5* (Washington, DC: Catholic University of America Press, 2001), 367.

36 "Our apostles also knew, through our Lord Jesus Christ, that there would be strife on account of the office of the episcopate. For this reason, therefore, inasmuch as they had obtained a perfect fore-knowledge of this, they appointed those [ministers] already mentioned, and afterwards gave instructions, that when these should fall asleep, other approved men should succeed them in their ministry" (1 Clement, 44).

37 Joseph M. Holden and Norman Geisler, *The Popular Handbook of Archaeology and the Bible* (Eugene, OR: Harvest House Publishers, 2013), 51.

38 Alan Shlemon, "Did Jesus Never Say Anything About Homosexuality?" (January 19, 2012), available online at: https://www.str.org/w/did-jesus-never-say-anything-about-homosexuality-.

39 Some Protestants claim that Paul gave the exact same teachings to his audience in both an oral and written form, so oral tradition is no longer necessary because its contents have been put into Scripture. But not only is this an unevidenced assumption, it is contradicted by Paul's own testimony about facts he reported to the Thessalonians that he did not reveal in his letters. See Trent Horn, *The Case for Catholicism* (San Francisco, CA: Ignatius Press, 2017), 39–40.

40 James White, *Scripture Alone* (Minneapolis, MN: Bethany House, 2004), 181.

41 Jerry Walls, "'If Christ Be not Raised'; If Peter Was Not the First Pope: Parallel Cases of Indispensable Doctrinal Foundations," *Journal of Biblical and Theological*

Studies vol. 4, no. 2 (2019), 254.

42 Joseph Barker, *A Review of the Bible* (London: Paternoster Row, 1848), 5.

43 *Summa Theologiae*, 1.68.3.

44 James White, *The Roman Catholic Controversy* (Minneapolis: Bethany House Publishers, 1996), 119.

45 The term is first used in Theophilus of Antioch's *To Autolycus*, book II. An early defense and explanation can be found in Tertullian's *Against Praxeas.*

46 "Not all the assertions of the teaching authority of the Church on questions of faith and morals are infallible and consequently irrevocable." Ludwig Ott, *Fundamentals of Catholic Dogma* (Charlotte, NC: TAN Books, 2009), 10.

47 The Congregation for the Doctrine of the Faith taught in *Donum Veritatis* that "the theologian knows that some judgments of the Magisterium could be justified at the time in which they were made, because while the pronouncements contained true assertions and others which were not sure, both types were inextricably connected. Only time has permitted discernment and, after deeper study, the attainment of true doctrinal progress" (24).

48 Norman L. Geisler and Ralph E. MacKenzie, *Roman Catholics and Evangelicals: Agreements and Differences* (Grand Rapids, MI: Baker Books, 1995), 216–217.

49 Norman Geisler and William Roach, *Defending Inerrancy: Affirming the Accuracy of Scripture for a New Generation* (Grand Rapids, MI: Baker Books, 2011), 296–302.

50 Josh McDowell, *The New Evidence That Demands a Verdict* (Nashville, TN: Thomas Nelson, 1999), 29.

51 Ron Rhodes, *Reasoning from the Scriptures with Catholics* (Eugene, OR: Harvest House Publishing, 2000), 37.

52 Gleason Archer, *New International Encyclopedia of Bible Difficulties* (Zondervan, 2011), kindle edition.

53 Norman L. Geisler and Thomas Howe, *The Big Book of Bible Difficulties* (Grand Rapids, MI: Baker Books, 1999), 15.

54 Gary Michuta, *Why Catholic Bibles are Bigger* (El Cajon, CA: Catholic Answers Press, 2017), 338.

55 "Do Protestants Have the Correct Old Testament Canon—Trent Horn vs Steve Christie Debate" (01:35:32), available online at: https://www.youtube.com/watch?v=mlCFhtSGK_w.

56 Trent Horn, *Hard Sayings: A Catholic Approach to Answering Bible Difficulties* (El Cajon, CA: Catholic Answers Press, 2016), 65–66.

57 H.T. Swan, "An Ancient Record of 'Couching' for Cataract," *Journal of the Royal Society of Medicine* vol. 88 (April 1995), 208–211.

58 Some may object that this isn't an error on par with the discrepancy in Judith because Mark is merely quoting what Jesus said and it may be the case that Jesus simply misremembered this historical detail that was part of his human knowledge. Setting aside the theological issues this raises about Jesus' knowledge of salvation history, one can find other examples of the protocanonical texts of the Bible themselves affirming historical difficulties, such as the well-known problem related to the census and the date of the death of Herod the Great. See Trent Horn, *Hard Sayings: A Catholic Approach to Answering Bible Difficulties* (El Cajon, CA: Catholic Answers Press, 2015), 117–122.

59 Daniel Wallace, "Mark 2:26 and the Problem of Abiathar," *Bible.org*, available online at: https://bible.org/article/mark-226-and-problem-abiathar.

60 "According to Hahn and Mitch in their commentary on Mark, Abiathar is infamous in Old Testament history as the last high priest of his line, who was banished from Jerusalem and the priesthood for opposing Solomon, the son of David and the heir of his kingdom (1 Kgs. 2:26–27). He thus represents the end of an old order that passes away with the coming of David's royal successor. . . . The Pharisees, then, represent an old order of covenant leadership that is about to expire, and if they persist in their opposition to Jesus, the new heir of the Davidic kingdom, they will meet the same disastrous fate that befell Abiathar."

61 Carey Moore, *Judith* (New York: Doubleday, 1985), 79.

62 See also K. Lawson Younger Jr., *Ancient Conquest Accounts: A Study in Ancient Near Eastern and Biblical History Writing* (Sheffield: Sheffield Academic Press, 1990), 219 and John H. Walton, "Joshua 10:12–15 and Mesopotamian Celestial Omen Texts," in *Faith, Tradition, and History: Old Testament Historiography in Its Near Eastern Context*, eds. A.R. Millard, J.K. Hoffmeier, and D.W. Baker (Winona Lake, IN: Eisenbrauns, 1994), 188.

63 See for example *New Approaches to the Book of Mormon: Explorations in Critical Methodology*, ed. Brent Lee Metcalfe (Salt Lake City: Signature Books, 1993).

64 William Sierichs Jr., "Daniel in the Historians' Den," *The Skeptical Review*

(July-August 1996), available online at: www.theskepticalreview.com/tsrmag/4danie96.html.

65 Jack Chick, "Why is Mary Crying?," available online at: https://www.chick.com/products/tract?stk=40.

66 Alexander Hislop, *The Two Babylons*, chapter III.

67 One popular atheist meme depicts a statue of an idol with the following text: "This is Ishtar, pronounced, 'Easter.' Easter was the original celebration of Ishtar, the Assyrian and Babylonian goddess of fertility and sex."

68 David Gange, "Religion and Science in Late Nineteenth-Century British Egyptology," *The Historical Journal* vol. 49, no. 4 (December 2006), 1101.

69 Jack Chick, *The Death Cookie*, available online at: https://www.chick.com/products/tract?stk=74.

70 Gerald Massey, *Ancient Egypt: The Light of the World* (London, T. Fisher Unwin, 1907), 221.

71 "During the seventh century, Irish missionaries, inspired by the Eastern monastic tradition, took to continental Europe the 'private' practice of penance, which does not require public and prolonged completion of penitential works before reconciliation with the Church. From that time on, the sacrament has been performed in secret between penitent and priest" (CCC 1447).

72 When it comes to Dionysus, I note in my book *Counterfeit Christs* that although Dionysus was a Greek god of wine and festivals, he is never said to have turned water into wine as Jesus did at the wedding of Cana. Instead, in one story he replaced the water in a spring with wine that tasted like water (so that he could rape a water nymph). According to New Testament scholar Carsten Claussen, "None of the scant supposed parallels from Hellenistic sources displays a changing of water into wine. The parallels are not close enough to explain the origin of the tradition behind John 2:1–11."

73 "The literary sources here are few but unmistakable: Mithra was known as the rock-born god." Manfred Clauss, *The Roman Cult of Mithras: The God and His Mysteries*, trans. Richard Gordon (New York: Routledge, 2001), 62.

74 T.N.D. Mettinger. *Riddle of Resurrection: "Dying and Rising Gods" in the Ancient Near East*, Coniectanea Biblica, Old Testament, 50 (Stockholm: Almqvist & Wiksell International, 2001), 221.

75 "Proven Truth: How Paganism and Idolatry Started in the Church," available online at: https://seekthegospeltruth.com/2020/08/02/proven-truth-how-paganism-and-idolatry-started-in-the-church/.

76 Ralph Woodrow, "The Two Babylons," *The Christian Research Institute* vol. 22, no. 2 (2000).

77 *Redemptoris Missio*, 52.

78 Jimmy Swaggart, *Jimmy Swaggart Bible Commentary: Luke* (Baton Rouge, LA Jimmy Swaggart Ministries, 2007), 72.

79 "Woman and man are to go to church decently attired, with natural step, embracing silence, possessing unfeigned love, pure in body, pure in heart, fit to pray to God." *The Instructor*, 3.11. Cited in Frank Viola and George Barna, Pagan Christianity?: Exploring the Roots of Our Church Practices (Wheaton, IL: Tyndale House Publishers, 2012), 12.

80 Philipp Schaff, *History of the Christian Church*, vol. III (New York: Charles Scribner's Sons, 1884), 396.

81 C.S. Lewis, *God in the Dock: Essays on Theology and Ethics*, ed. Walter Hooper (Grand Rapids, MI: William B. Eerdmans, 2014), 59.

82 Michael Horton, "Gnostic Worship," *Modern Reformation* vol. 4 (July/August 1995), 14.

83 William Webster, *The Church of Rome at the Bar of History* (Carlisle, PA: Banner of Truth, 1995), 95.

84 Geisler and MacKenzie, *Roman Catholics and Evangelicals*, (Grand Rapids, MI: Baker Books, 1995) 293.

85 William Webster, *The Church of Rome at the Bar of History* (Carlisle, PA: Banner of Truth, 1995), 81

86 Harry Emerson Fosdick, "Shall the Fundamentalists Win?," available online at: http://historymatters.gmu.edu/d/5070/.

87 Bart Ehrman, *How Jesus Became God*, (New York: Harper One, 2014), 238.

88 Richard Carrier, *On the Historicity of Jesus, Why We Might Have Reason for Doubt* (United Kingdom: Sheffield Phoenix Press, 2014) 515.

89 See F.B.A. Asiedu, *Josephus, Paul, and the Fate of Early Christianity: History and Silence in the First Century* (United Kingdom: Lexington Books/Fortress Academic, 2019).

90 Timothy and Lydia Mcgrew, "The Argument from Miracles," in *The Blackwell Companion to Natural Theology*, eds. William Lane Craig and J.P. Moreland (West Sussex: Blackwell, 2009), 598.

91 "The existence of the works of Thucydides, for example, is not noted by any author whose works we now possess until 250 years after they were written. Grafton's *Chronicles*, which embrace the reign of King John, make no reference to *Magna Carta*. In the extensive memoirs of Ulysses Grant, Lincoln's general during the American Civil War, there is no mention of the Emancipation Proclamation. Neither Herodotus nor Thucydides, nor any of their contemporaries mentions Rome, even in passing, a point Josephus brings up in his controversy with Apion. In his sprawling travelogue, Marco Polo never refers to the Great Wall of China, or tea, or printed books. Examples of this sort could be multiplied almost endlessly." Timothy McGrew, "Arguments from Providence and from Miracles" in *Two Dozen (or so) Arguments for God: The Plantinga Project*, eds. Jerry Walls and Trent Dougherty (Oxford: Oxford University Press, 2018), 347.

92 Charles Augustus Briggs, "The Virgin Birth of Our Lord," *The American Journal of Theology* vol. 12, no. 2 (April 1908), 189–210, available online at: https://www.jstor.org/stable/3155127?seq=2#metadata_info_tab_contents.

93 J. Gresham Machen, "The Virgin Birth," *The Bible Today*, 19.3 (December 1924), 75–79.

94 See for example Letter to the Smyrnaeans, 8 and Letter to the Trallians, 2.

95 *Against Heresies*, 3.3.3. Some Protestants might respond by saying that Irenaeus is not giving a historical account and that the silence in Ignatius on the bishop of Rome still compromises the evidence for the papacy. If they go that route, however, I wonder how they would answer critics who say Paul only had a hallucinatory vision of Jesus. After all, when Paul recounts his conversion story in Galatians, he doesn't mention the conversion on the Damascus road found in Acts.

96 Michael J. Kruger, "Gospel Critics and the Argument from Silence," available online at: https://www.biblestudytools.com/blogs/michael-j-kruger/gospel-critics-and-the-argument-from-silence.html.

97 F.F. Bruce, *The Canon of Scripture* (Downers Grove, IL: IVP Academic, 1988), 129.

98 Matt Emerson, "Arguing from Silence in the Early Church" (September

15, 2017), available online at: https://secundumscripturas.com/2017/09/15/arguing-from-silence-in-the-early-church/.

99 Geisler and MacKenzie, *Roman Catholics and Evangelicals*, (Grand Rapids, MI: Baker Books, 1995), 502.

100 John Jefferson Davis, "The Perseverance of the Saints: A History of the Doctrine," *Journal of the Evangelical Theological Society* vol. 34, no. 2 (June 1991).

101 Matt Emerson, "Arguing from Silence in the Early Church" (September 15, 2017), available online at: https://secundumscripturas.com/2017/09/15/arguing-from-silence-in-the-early-church/.

102 One scholar says the seventeenth-century German pastor Joachim Betkius "traced the decline of the Christian church to the time when Christians were first granted toleration in the Roman Empire. The reason for this decline was that the security under the Christian emperors opened the doors to opportunists and fair weather converts, who would never have endured the trials of the pagan era." Thomas Ahnert, "Historicizing Heresy in the Early German Enlightenment," in *Heresy in Transition: Transforming Ideas of Heresy in Medieval and Early Modern Europe*, eds. John Christian Laursen and Cary J. Nederman (New York: Routledge, 2005), 135.

103 Paul V.M. Flesher, "UW Religion Today: How Constantine Created the Christian Church" (February 4, 2015), available online at: https://www.uwyo.edu/uw/news/2015/02/uw-religion-today-how-constantine-created-the-christian-church.html.

104 Dan Brown, *The Da Vinci Code* (New York: Random House, 2003), 306.

105 Bart D. Ehrman, *Truth and Fiction in The Da Vinci Code* (New York: Oxford University Press, 2004), 15.

106 Ignatius of Antioch, *Letter to the Ephesians*, 18 and Apology of Aristedes, 2.

107 Robert Van Voorst, *Jesus Outside the New Testament: An Introduction to the Ancient Evidence* (Grand Rapids: Wm. B. Eerdmans, 2000), 58.

108 Peter Keegan, *Graffiti in Antiquity* (New York: Routledge, 2014), 108.

109 Mary Ann Collins, Catholic Concerns: Where Does the Road to Rome Lead? (Bloomington, IN: iUniverse, 2008), 94.

110 Josh McDowell, *The Da Vinci Code: A Quest for Answers* (Holiday, FL: Green Key Books, 2006), electronic edition.

111 For a recent treatment see Joseph Heschmeyer, *The Early Church Was the Catholic Church: The Catholic Witness of the Fathers in Christianity's First Two Centuries* (El Cajon, CA: Catholic Answers Press, 2021).

112 *Epistle to the Smyrnaeans*, 7.

113 *First Apology*, 66.

114 Robert Van Voorst, *Jesus Outside the New Testament: An Introduction to the Ancient Evidence* (Grand Rapids: Wm. B. Eerdmans, 2000), 24. The third-century Christian author Minucius Felix says the story of Christians ritualistically killing and eating babies is "as much to be detested as it is well known" (*Octavius*, 9).

115 Frank Viola and George Barna, *Pagan Christianity?: Exploring the Roots of Our Church Practices* (Wheaton, IL: Tyndale House Publishers, 2012), 13.

116 Justin Martyr said this prophecy was fulfilled when Christians "in every place offer sacrifices to him, i.e., the bread of the Eucharist, and also the cup of the Eucharist" (*Dialogue with Trypho*, 41). Indeed, Justin's description of Christian liturgy in his letter to the Roman emperor closely parallels elements that are still found in the Catholic Mass, such as the prayers of the faithful, the exchange of peace, and the "great amen" (along with the consecration of bread and wine). While discussing the Last Supper, Irenaeus said Christ "gives us as the means of subsistence the first-fruits of his own gifts in the New Testament, concerning which Malachi, among the twelve prophets, thus spoke beforehand" (*Against Heresies*, 4.17.5).

117 *Epistle 62.14*.

118 William Webster, *The Church of Rome at the Bar of History* (Carlisle, PA: Banner of Truth Trust, 1995), 126.

119 Gregory Koukl, *Tactics* (Grand Rapids: Zondervan, 2009), 183.

120 Dan Brown, *The Da Vinci Code* (New York: Random House, 2003), 308. The novel's historian also conflates these documents with the Dead Sea Scrolls, further demonstrating Brown's tenuous grasp of the relevant historical material.

121 Against those who claim Protestants have always existed and were identified as medieval heretics see James Edward McGoldrick's *Baptist Successionism: A Crucial Question in Baptist History* (1994).

122 Michael Davies, "Annibale Bugnini: The main author of the *Novus Ordo*," available online at: http://www.catholicapologetics.info/modernproblems/newmass/bugnini.html.

123 Marian T. Horvat, "Two Sister Lucys of Fatima?," available online at: https://www.traditioninaction.org/HotTopics/g11htTwoSisterLucys_Horvat.htm.

124 Traditio Fathers, "John Paul I May Have Been the 'Traditional' Pope Prayed For | The Arguably-assassinated Pope Was Reportedly About to Restore the Traditional Latin Mass," available online at: http://www.traditio.com/comment/com1106.htm#110627.

125 Kaleigh Rogers and Jasmine Mithani, "Why People Fall For Conspiracy Theories" (June 15, 2021), available online at: https://fivethirtyeight.com/features/why-people-fall-for-conspiracy-theories/.

126 *Etsi Multa* 22.

127 *Satis Cognitum* 3.

128 William Webster, *The Church of Rome at the Bar of History* (Carlisle, PA: Banner of Truth Trust, 1995), 62.

129 Gregg Allison, *40 Questions about Roman Catholicism* (Grand Rapids: Kregel Publications, 2021), 23.

130 Joseph Wheless, *Forgery in Christianity* (New York: Alfred A Knopf, 1930), vii.

131 Bart Ehrman, *Forgery and Counterforgery: The Use of Literary Deceit in Early Christian Polemics* (New York: Oxford University Press, 2013), 1.

132 Dan Barker, *Godless: How an Evangelical Preacher Became One of America's Leading Atheists* (Berkeley, CA: Ulysses Press, 2008), 255.

133 Tertullian references the darkening of the sun at the Crucifixion, saying, "Those who were not aware that this had been predicted about Christ, no doubt thought it an eclipse. You yourselves have the account of the world-portent still in your archives." He then writes, "All these things Pilate did to Christ; and now in fact a Christian in his own convictions, he sent word of him to the reigning Cæsar, who was at the time Tiberius" (*Apology*, 21).

134 See Bart Ehrman and Zlatko Plese, *The Apocryphal Gospels: Texts and Translations* (New York: Oxford University Press, 2011), 491–500.

135 Richard Carrier, "The Historicity of Paul the Apostle" (June 6, 2015), available online at: https://www.richardcarrier.info/archives/7643.

136 Ignaz von Döllinger, *The Pope and the Council* (London: Rivingtons, 1869), 95.

137 *Church History*, 2.9.

138 "What is the 'Johannine Gloss,'" available online at: https://www.catholic.com/

qa/what-is-the-johannine-gloss.

139 "This decree was passed to check the audacity of private teachers who attributed to themselves the right either of rejecting entirely the authenticity of the Johannine comma, or at least of calling it into question by their own final judgment. But it was not meant at all to prevent Catholic writers from investigating the subject more fully and, after weighing the arguments accurately on both sides, with that and temperance which the gravity of the subject requires, from inclining toward an opinion in opposition to its authenticity, provided they professed that they were ready to abide by the judgment of the Church, to which the duty was delegated by Jesus Christ not only of interpreting holy Scripture but also of guarding it faithfully" (Denzinger, 3682).

140 See for example the numerous citations in *Keys Over the Christian World* by Scott Butler and Collorari.

141 "The task of portraying Jesus for a Protestant market, which was increasingly shaped by the visual rhetoric of photography, found textual support in a medieval manuscript that purported to be (and was long respected as) a description of Jesus by a contemporary." David Morgan, *Protestants and Pictures: Religion, Visual Culture, and the Age of American Mass Production* (New York: Oxford University Press, 1999), 283.

142 James R. White, *Mary: Another Redeemer?* (Bloomington, MN: Bethany House, 1998), 54.

143 Norman Davies, *Europe: A History* (New York: Oxford University Press, 1996), 260.

144 "For, since you are subject to the bishop as to Jesus Christ, you appear to me to live not after the manner of men, but according to Jesus Christ, who died for us, in order, by believing in his death, you may escape from death. It is therefore necessary that, as you indeed do, so without the bishop you should do nothing, but should also be subject to the presbytery, as to the apostle of Jesus Christ, who is our hope, in whom, if we live, we shall [at last] be found. It is fitting also that the deacons, as being [the ministers] of the mysteries of Jesus Christ, should in every respect be pleasing to all. For they are not ministers of meat and drink, but servants of the Church of God. They are bound, therefore, to avoid all grounds of accusation [against them], as they would do fire (Letter to the Trallians, 2).

145 Philip Schaff *History of the Christian Church* vol. II (New York: Charles Scribner's Sons, 1883).

146 Jaroslav Pelikan, *Development of Christian Doctrine: Some Historical Prolegomena* (New Haven: Yale University Press, 1969), 58.

147 Klemens Löffler, "Joseph Georg Strossmayer," *The Catholic Encyclopedia*, vol. 14. (New York: Robert Appleton Company, 1912).

148 Ante Kadić, "Bishop Strossmayer and the First Vatican Council," *The Slavonic and East European Review* vol. 49, no. 116 (July 1971), 385.

149 Gary Metz, "Jack Chick's Anti-Catholic *Alberto* Comic Book Is Exposed as a Fraud," *Christianity Today* (March 13, 1981), available online at: https://www.christianitytoday.com/ct/1981/march-13/jack-chicks-anti-catholic-alberto-comic-book-is-exposed-as.html.

150 *Summa Contra Gentiles* 1.6.1.

151 John Calvin, *Institutions of the Christian Religion*, preface, available online at: https://sourcebooks.fordham.edu/source/calvin-onclergy.asp.

152 Thomas S. Kidd, "The Healing of Mercy Wheeler: Illness and Miracles Among Early American Evangelicals," *The William and Mary Quarterly* Third Series, vol. 63, no. 1 (January 2006), 149–170.

153 Jon Mark Ruthven, *On the Cessation of the Charismata: The Protestant Polemic on Post-biblical Miracles* (Tulsa, OK: Word and Spirit Press, 2011), 27.

154 In addition, some Protestants believe that only certain types of miracles have continued into the post-apostolic age; and many other Protestants describe themselves as "open, but cautious" regarding post-apostolic miracle claims. For a general overview and interaction between these views, see *Are Miraculous Gifts for Today?: 4 Views* (2011) published by Zondervan Academic.

155 Richard B. Gaffin Jr., "A Cessationist View," in *Are Miraculous Gifts for Today?: 4 Views*, ed. Stanley Gundry (Grand Rapids, MI: Zondervan, 1996), 28.

156 Jack Deere, *Surprised by the Power of the Spirit* (Grand Rapids, MI: Zondervan, 1993), 268.

157 B.B. Warfield, *Counterfeit Miracles* (New York: Charles Scribner's Sons, 1918), 100.

158 Ibid., 66.

159 "What am I to do? I am so pressed by the promise of finishing this work, that I cannot record all the miracles I know; and doubtless several of our adherents,

when they read what I have narrated, will regret that I have omitted so many which they, as well as I, certainly know. Even now I beg these persons to excuse me, and to consider how long it would take me to relate all those miracles, which the necessity of finishing the work I have undertaken forces me to omit" (*City of God*, 22.8).

160 "The miracle which was wrought at Milan when I was there, and by which a blind man was restored to sight, could come to the knowledge of many; for not only is the city a large one, but also the emperor was there at the time, and the occurrence was witnessed by an immense concourse of people that had gathered to the bodies of the martyrs Protasius and Gervasius, which had long lain concealed and unknown, but were now made known to the bishop Ambrose in a dream, and discovered by him. By virtue of these remains the darkness of that blind man was scattered, and he saw the light of day" (ibid.).

161 "It is a very disturbing fact further that the very Fathers who record long lists of miracles contemporary with themselves, yet betray a consciousness that miracles had nevertheless, in some sense or other, ceased with the apostolic age." B.B. Warfield, *Counterfeit Miracles* (New York: Charles Scribner's Sons, 1918), 46.

162 L. Philip Barnes, "Miracles, Charismata and Benjamin B. Warfield" vol. 67, no. 3 (1995), 229–230.

163 Cited in B.B. Warfield, *Counterfeit Miracles* (New York: Charles Scribner's Sons, 1918), 58.

164 Michael R. Licona, *The Resurrection of Jesus: A New Historiographical Approach* (Downer's Grove, IL: Intervarsity Press, 2010), 486.

165 Hector Avalos, *The End of Biblical Studies* (Amherst, NY: Prometheus Books, 2007), 193.

166 Bart Ehrman, *How Jesus Became God* (New York: Harper One, 2014), 199.

167 Dwight Longenecker and David Gustafson, *Mary: A Catholic Evangelical Debate* (Brazos Press, 2003), 140.

168 Elliot Miller and Kenneth R. Samples, *The Cult of the Virgin: Catholic Mariology and the Apparitions of Mary* (Grand Rapids. MI: Baker Publishing, 1992), 129.

169 Richard Dawkins, *The God Delusion* (New York: Bantam Press, 2006), 91. Dawkins goes on to write, "But it is even harder to accept that it really happened without the rest of the world, outside Fatima, seeing it too—and not

just seeing it, but feeling it as the catastrophic destruction of the solar system, including acceleration forces sufficient to hurl everybody into space" (92). But Dawkins has overlooked another possibility: God miraculously caused people in Fatima to see an optical spectacle, as well as other effects (like soaking clothes drying instantly), as a "local miracle" that was accomplished without changing the location of the sun or earth in orbit.

170 Michael Licona, "#581 Appearances of Mary and Jesus' Resurrection Appearances" (June 3, 2018), available online at: https://www.reasonablefaith.org/writings/question-answer/appearances-of-mary-and-jesus-resurrection-appearances.

171 Michael R. Licona, *The Resurrection of Jesus: A New Historiographical Approach* (Downer's Grove, IL: Intervarsity Press, 2010), 491.

172 Interestingly, the most popular naturalistic explanation for the events at Fatima comes from a Catholic scholar, Fr. Stanley Jaki. He proposes a combination of meteorological effects like reflective ice crystals, temperature inversion, and damage caused by starting at the sun causing observers to imagine the sun changing color and moving erratically. Fr. Jaki agrees the crowd saw something, but he believes they may have had a misperception rather than a hallucination. For a critique of this hypothesis, see Tyler Dalton McNabb and Joseph E. Blado, "Mary And Fátima: A Modest C-Inductive Argument For Catholicism," *Perichoresis* vol. 18, no. 5 (2020), 59–61.

173 Michael Licona, "#581 Appearances of Mary and Jesus' Resurrection Appearances" (June 3, 2018), available online at: https://www.reasonablefaith.org/writings/question-answer/appearances-of-mary-and-jesus-resurrection-appearances.

174 "The Papists, especially Eisengrein who published the miracles at Altötting, should recognize that this story sounds exactly like the false appearance described in 1 Samuel 29. This Mary of whom he [Eisengrein] speaks was not the holy Virgin Mary, Christ our Lord's mother. Rather she was a false Mary whom the Jesuits conjured up with the form and the appearance of the Holy Virgin Mary. [This they performed] through their sorcery and the company that they keep with the devil. Just like the devil's whore and soothsayer conjured up through her swearing and magic not Samuel, but the devil himself brought up from hell in the form of Samuel." Cited in Philip M. Soergel, *Wondrous in His Saints: Counter-Reformation Propaganda in Bavaria* (Los Angeles: University of California Press, 1993), 135.

175 "Doctrine of Creation (Part 17)" (December 23, 2012), available online at: https://www.reasonablefaith.org/podcasts/defenders-podcast-series-2/creation-and-evolution-part-7/doctrine-of-creation-part-17.

176 The devil is certainly clever, and in any given instance he could have a long-term plan to harm souls that has intermediate steps that include people (temporarily) returning to the true Church. But historical instances of false Marian apparitions show this is not the case and that such events tend to almost immediately entice people to pursue evil practices or disobey representatives of the true Church. See for example Bp. Francis Mugavero of Brooklyn's statement denouncing the so-called "Bayside apparitions," available online at: https://www.ewtn.com/catholicism/library/declaration-concerning-the-bayside-movement-11313.

177 "Prefatory Address to His Most Christian Majesty, the Most Mighty and Illustrious Monarch, Francis, King of the French," available online at: https://www.ccel.org/ccel/calvin/institutes.ii.viii.html

178 Tyler Dalton McNabb and Joseph E. Blado, "Mary And Fátima: A Modest C-Inductive Argument For Catholicism," *Perichoresis* vol. 18, no. 5 (2020), 62.

179 John Calvin, "Calvin: Letter to the King [on the Clergy]," available online at: https://sourcebooks.fordham.edu/source/calvin-onclergy.asp.

180 See R.W. Scribner, "Incombustible Luther: The Image of the Reformer in Early Modern Germany," *Past & Present*, no. 110 (February 1986), 38–68.

181 This can be found in the tract "My Name? . . . In the Vatican?" See also, Jimmy Akin, "Meet Jack Chick," *Catholic Answers Magazine* (2004), available online at: catholic.com/magazine/print-edition/meet-jack-chick.

182 Jimmy Swaggart, *Catholicism and Christianity* (Baton Rouge, LA: Jimmy Swaggart Ministries, 1986). 31.

183 William Edward Hartpole Lecky, *History of the Rise and Influence of the Spirit of Rationalism in Europe*, vol. 2 (London: Longmans, Green, and Co., 1866), 35.

184 Richard Dawkins, *The God Delusion* (London: Bantam Press, 2006), 257.

185 "In no real as opposed to nominal sense, then, was he a Christian." Christopher Hitchens, *God Is Not Great: How Religion Poisons Everything* (New York: Hachette Group, 2007), 176.

186 Lee Strobel, *The Case for Faith* (Grand Rapids: Zondervan, 2021), 219.

187 Ibid., 225.

188 Kyle J. Gerkin, "Objections Sustained!," *The Secular Web* (January 1, 2001), available online at: https://infidels.org/library/modern/kyle-gerkin-objections-sustained-obj7/.

189 Johannes Janssen, *History of the German People from the Close of the Middle Ages*, vol. 10 (St. Louis: B. Herder, 1910), 222–223. This quote is often incorrectly attributed to Martin Luther. Protestant author James Swan says, "The error of attributing this writing to Luther is throughout the Internet. Whoever originally swiped this quote from Janssen (and I'm fairly certain I know who that was) never bothered to look the quote up to check it. Hence there are now all sorts of web pages claiming Luther wrote it. Shame on Rome's apologists, once again. What can be said of it is that Luther and the other Wittenberg theologians signed the document in agreement with what Melanchthon had penned." James Swan, "Follow-up: The 38 Most Ridiculous Things Martin Luther Ever Wrote?" (September 18, 2013), available online at: https://beggarsallreformation.blogspot.com/2013/09/follow-upthe-38-most-ridiculous-things.html.

190 Charles Phillips and Alan Axelrod, *Encyclopedia of Wars*, vol. 3 (New York: Facts on File, 2005), 1484–1485.

191 Edward Peters, *Inquisition* (Berkeley: University of California Press, 1989), 87.

192 Gregory Koukl, *Tactics: A Game Plan for Discussing Your Christian Convictions* (Grand Rapids: Zondervan, 2009), 182.

193 Tim Challies, "The Mischievous Protestant's Guide to Catholic Rome" (June 9, 2017), available online at: https://www.challies.com/articles/the-mischievous-protestants-guide-to-rome/.

194 Steve Wells, "Exodus 16," *The Skeptic's Annotated Bible*, available online at: https://skepticsannotatedbible.com/ex/16.html.

195 Tim Challies, "The Servetus Problem" (September 19, 2005), available online: https://www.challies.com/articles/the-servetus-problem/.

196 Kent R. Hill, *The Soviet Union on the Brink: An Inside Look at Christianity & Glasnost* (Portland, OR: Multnomah, 1991), 83.

197 Gregory Koukl, *Tactics: A Game Plan for Discussing Your Christian Convictions* (Grand Rapids: Zondervan, 2009), 177.

198 Dinesh D'Souza, "Atheism, Not Religion, Is the Real Force Behind the Mass Murders of History," *The Christian Science Monitor* (November 21, 2006), available

online at: https://www.csmonitor.com/2006/1121/p09s01-coop.html.

199 Adolf Hitler cited Christianity in his speeches, though that may have been a calculated ploy to garner support from religious Germans. My colleague Jimmy Akin has said that "if we had to describe Hitler's religious views in a single phrase, we could say that he was a pseudo-scientific evolutionary pantheist."

200 Stephen Van Eck, "Rogue's Gallery: Know the Popes!," *The Secular Web* (July 12, 2014), available online: https://infidels.org/kiosk/article/rogue-s-gallery-know-the-popes/.

201 Thomas Paine, *Age of Reason*, 1.4.

202 Jeffrey Jay Lowder, "Are Christians the Best Argument Against Christianity?" *The Secular Frontier* (August 6, 2012), available online at: https://secularfrontier.infidels.org/2012/08/are-christians-the-best-argument-against-christianity/.

203 Jerry L. Walls, "The Problem of Bad Popes: The Argument from Conspicuous Corruption," *Perichoresis* vol. 18, no. 5 (2020), 94.

204 Francis X. Rocca, *Suspense, Planning during Interregnum*, March 6, 2013, available online at: https://thetablet.org/suspense-planning-during-interregnum/.

205 Molinism is an approach to understanding God's foreknowledge and human freedom derived from the work of the sixteenth-century Spanish Jesuit Luis de Molina. For a defense of this view, see Thomas Flint's *Divine Providence: The Molinist Account* (1998) and William Lane Craig's *The Only Wise God* (1999).

206 Thomas P. Flint, *Divine Providence: The Molinist Account* (New York: Cornell University Press, 1998), 184.

207 Jerry L. Walls "The Problem of Bad Popes: The Argument From Conspicuous Corruption" *Perichoresis*, vol. 18, no. 5 (2020), 102.

208 John W. Loftus, *Why I Became an Atheist* (New York: Prometheus Book, 2012), Kindle edition.

209 Ibid., 103.

210 Jerry Walls and David Baggett, *Good God: The Theistic Foundations of Morality* (Oxford: Oxford University Press, 2012), 153.

211 Cited in Robert Michael, *Holy Hatred: Christianity, Antisemitism, and the Holocaust* (New York: Palgrave Macmillan, 2006), 113.

212 Konrad Szocik and Philip L. Walden, "The Attitude of the Catholic Church Toward the Jews: An Outline of a Turbulent History," *Numen* vol. 64, no. 2/3 (2017).

213 *Against the Jews*, 1.6

214 John P. Meier, "The Brothers and Sisters of Jesus in Ecumenical Perspective," *The Catholic Biblical Quarterly* vol. 54, no. 1 (January 1992), 27.

215 James White, "The Unity and Certainty of Rome" (August 10, 2009), available online at: https://www.aomin.org/aoblog/roman-catholicism/the-unity-and-certainty-of-rome/.

216 For example, in his massive treatment of the birth of Jesus, Brown says, "The scientifically controllable biblical evidence leaves the question of the historicity of the virginal conception unresolved." Raymond E. Brown, *The Birth of the Messiah: A Commentary on the Infancy Narratives in the Gospels of Matthew and Luke* (New York: Doubleday, 1993), 698. In another work, he says the doctrine of the virginal conception of Jesus is one "for which there is slender basis in Scripture." Raymond E. Brown, *Biblical Exegesis and Church Doctrine*, (New York: Paulist Press, 1985), 34.

217 John Loftus, "Christian Scholarship Led Me to Reject Christianity," *Debunking Christianity* (November 18, 2006), available online at: https://www.debunking-christianity.com/2006/11/.

218 William Lane Craig, "'*Noli me tangere*': Why John Meier Won't Touch the Risen Lord," *Heythrop Journal* vol. 50, no. 1 (2009), 91–97.

219 John P. Meier, *A Marginal Jew*, vol. 1, p. 221, cited in https://www.patheos.com/blogs/radicalchristianmillennial/2016/08/the-virgin-birth-is-sexist/.

220 "Debate: Is the New Testament We Possess Today Inspired? (White vs Ally)" 33:25, available online at: https://www.youtube.com/watch?v=2T0RvFEDK70&t=2015s.

221 James White, "A Post and Pre Debate Note to Shabir Ally" (October 8, 2013), available online: https://www.aomin.org/aoblog/islam/a-post-and-pre-debate-note-to-shabir-ally/. In his book *Scripture Alone*, White answers an interlocutor who says, "Even Christian scholars admit the Bible has inconsistent teaching on basic issues" by saying, "I see you've been doing some reading in postmodern humanist liberal theology—what a combination!" (165).

222 "For those not familiar with Roman Catholic scholarship, Brown and Fitzmyer are names at the very top of Rome's NT scholarship list over the past thirty years, both having worked and published at the direction of high-level papal commissions, etc. The *Jerome Biblical Commentary* is likewise Roman Catholic,

so to find it contradicting Ray's surface-level comments on the text is a bit humorous." James White, "Brown and Fitzmyer vs. Ray" (December 22, 2007), available online at: https://www.aomin.org/aoblog/roman-catholicism/brown-and-fitzmyer-vs-ray/.

223 "The Great Debate VI, Purgatory—Stravinskas" (May 31, 2001), 45:04, available online at: https://www.youtube.com/watch?v=PtAkuMs54qM.

224 Anna Quindlen, "To the Altar" *The Baltimore Sun* (June 6, 1994), available online at: https://www.baltimoresun.com/news/bs-xpm-1994-06-07-1994158170-story.html.

225 National Council of Catholic Bishops's Committee, "Review of Fr. McBrien's *Catholicism*" (April 9, 1996), available online at: https://www.catholicculture.org/culture/library/view.cfm?id=541&CFID=121743&CFTOKEN=22026492.

226 James White, *The Roman Catholic Controversy* (Minneapolis: Bethany House Publishers, 1996), 120.

227 Luke Rivington, *Authority: A Plain Reason for Joining the Church of Rome* (London: Kegan, Paul, Trench, Trubner, & Co., 1890), 35.

228 A. Edward Siecienski, *The Papacy and the Orthodox: Sources and History of a Debate* (New York: Oxford University Press, 2017), 126.

229 Cited in Scott Butler and John Collorafi, *Keys over the Christian World* (State Line, PA: Catholic Apologetics International Publishing Inc., 2021), 603. Another translation renders the passage this way: "That great one, Peter, however, did not progress toward this grace bit by bit but at one and the same moment heard his brother and believed in the Lamb and was perfected by faith and, having attached himself to the Rock, became a rock." Gregory of Nyssa, *Homily on the Song of Songs*, trans. Richard A. Norris, Jr. (Atlanta: Society of Biblical Literature, 2012), 459.

230 See for example James White, *Scripture Alone* (Bloomington, MN: Bethany House, 2004), 106–108.

231 Michael J. Kruger, *The Question of Canon* (Downer's Grove, IL: InterVarsity Press, 2013).

232 Jerry L. Walls, "'If Christ Be Not Raised'; If Peter Was Not the First Pope: Parallel Cases of Indispensable Doctrinal Foundations," *Journal of Biblical and Theological Studies* vol. 4, no. 2, (2019), 253.

233 "The STRONGEST Argument Against Catholicism w/ Dr. Jerry Walls" 19:35, available online at: https://www.youtube.com/watch?v=DgtyTtGlGrQ .

234 Jerry L. Walls and Kenneth J. Collins, *Roman but Not Catholic: What Remains at Stake 500 Years after the Reformation* (Grand Rapids MI: Baker Academic, 2017), 21.

235 Eamon Duffy, *The Creed in the Catechism* (New York: Continuum, 1996), 18.

236 Marjorie Hyer, "Vatican Rules Kung Guilty of Heresy," *The Washington Post* (December 19, 1979), available online at: https://www.washingtonpost.com/archive/politics/1979/12/19/vatican-rules-kung-guilty-of-heresy/fa2c354f-7379-49b6-bea5-3db7689480d2/.

237 "DEBATE: Dan Barker vs. Mike Licona (Did Jesus Rise from the dead?—2003)" (01:29:45), available online at: https://www.youtube.com/watch?v=0IA5Gko-vFg.

238 *Will the Real Jesus Please Stand Up? A Debate Between William Lane Craig and John Dominic Crossan*, ed. Paul Copan (Grand Rapids: Baker Books, 1998), 50–51.

239 Peter Enns, *The Sin of Certainty: Why God Desires Our Trust More Than Our "Correct" Beliefs* (New York: Harper One, 2016), 48–49.

240 Matthew Barrett, "Sola Scriptura in the Strange Land of Evangelicalism: The Peculiar but Necessary Responsibility of Defending Sola Scriptura Against Our Own Kind," *SBJT* vol. 19, no. 4 (2015), 9–38.

241 John Ankerberg and John Weldon, *Protestants & Catholics—Do They Now Agree?* (Harvard House Publishers, 1995), 109.

242 Alphonsus Liguori, *The Glories of Mary* (London: Burns and Oates, 1868), 112.

243 Diana Fishlock, "Atheist Group's Slavery Billboard in Harrisburg Offends African-Americans" *Penn Live* (March 6, 2012), available online at: https://www.pennlive.com/midstate/2012/03/post_325.html.

244 Jonathan Edwards, "Sinners in the Hands of an Angry God" (1741), available online at: https://www.blueletterbible.org/Comm/edwards_jonathan/Sermons/Sinners.cfm.

245 Keith Parsons, "Hell: Christianity's Most Damnable Doctrine," in *The End of Christianity*, ed. John W. Loftus (New York: Prometheus Books, 2011), 237.

246 James White, *The Roman Catholic Controversy* (Minneapolis: Bethany House Publishers, 1996), 181.

247 "St. Patrick's Purgatory," in *Visions of Heaven and Hell Before Dante*, ed. Eileen Gardiner (New York: Italica Press, 1989), 137–141.

248 "Can a Loving God Send People to Hell? The Craig-Bradley Debate" (January 1994), available online at: https://www.reasonablefaith.org/media/debates/can-a-loving-god-send-people-to-hell-the-craig-bradley-debate. References to Fr. Furniss can also be found in George H. Smith, *Atheism: The Case Against God* (New York: Prometheus Books, 1989), 299–300.

249 Against Edward's view of God dangling us over a fiery furnace like a spider on a string, C.S. Lewis imagined hell being like a perpetually drab city whose residents hate each other so much they constantly move away from each other further and further into isolation. One essay on the official C.S. Lewis website says, "Separation seems for Lewis to describe the essential idea of hell, capturing what is conveyed by the biblical imagery of torture, destruction, and privation. To be forever cut off from God's presence, eternally unable to know God's love and mercy, would be a torture best described by being burned ceaselessly by fire." "Heaven and Hell as an Idea and Image in C.S. Lewis," available online at: https://www.cslewis.com/heaven-and-hell-as-idea-and-image-in-c-s-lewis.

250 Joseph Cardinal Ratzinger, *Eschatology: Death and Eternal Life*, 2nd ed. (Washington, DC: Catholic University of America Press, 2007), 230. Cited in Jimmy Akin, "How to Explain Purgatory to Protestants," available online at: http://jimmyakin.com/how-to-explain-purgatory-to-protestants.

251 Dan Barker, "With Perfect Hatred" (July 1991), available online at: https://ffrf.org/component/k2/item/18421-with-perfect-hatred.

252 Norman Geisler and Thomas Howe, *The Big Book of Bible Difficulties* (Grand Rapids, MI: Baker Books, 1992), 333.

253 D.A. Carson, "Worship Under the Word," in *Worship by the Book*, ed. D.A. Carson (Grand Rapids, MI: Zondervan, 2002), 26.

254 Alphonsus Liguori, *The Glories of Mary* (London: Burns and Oates, 1868), 112.

255 St. Louis de Montfort, *True Devotion to the Blessed Virgin Mary,* trans. Fr. Frederick William Faber (Charlotte, NC: TAN Books, 2010), 140.

256 Timothy Kauffman, "'We Don't Worship Mary'" Part 2" (June 14, 2015), available online at: https://www.whitehorseblog.com/2014/06/15/we-dont-worship-mary-pt2/.

257 St. Louis de Montfort, *True Devotion to Mary*, trans. Fr. Frederick William Faber (Charlotte, NC: TAN Books, 2010), 7.

258 "Through baptism these people threw out unbelief, had their unclean way of life washed away, and entered into a pure life of faith and love. Now they fall away into unbelief and . . . soil themselves again in filth." *Luther's Works*, 30:190.

259 Eric Metaxas, *Martin Luther: The Man Who Rediscovered God and Changed the World* (New York: Viking, 2017), 257–258.

260 Joseph F. Smith, John R. Winder, and Anthon H. Lund, "Origin of Man," *Improvement Era*, (November 1909), 75–81, available online at: https://www.churchofjesuschrist.org/study/ensign/2002/02/the-origin-of-man?lang=eng.

261 Brigham Young, *Journal of Discourses*, 8:115.

262 "Pascal's Wager," available online at: https://spot.colorado.edu/~heathwoo/Phil383/pascal.htm.

263 You find this same "happiness gap" in many other countries, including Japan, Germany, Peru, and Australia ("Are Religious People Happier, Healthier?," (2019), available online at: https://www.pewresearch.org/fact-tank/2019/01/31/are-religious-people-happier-healthier-our-new-global-study-explores-this-question/).

264 *Ad Petri Cathedram*, 72.

265 C.S. Lewis, *Mere Christianity* (New York: Harper Collins, 1952), 162.